Wally Gilbert

From
Science
To
Art

An Exhibition

at

San Diego City College
May 18th, 2019 – July 25, 2019

City Gallery, AH 314

1508 C Street

San Deigo, CA 92101

Catalogue of Images

Wally Gilbert

From
Science
To
Art

Curated by
Chang and Jae Kim

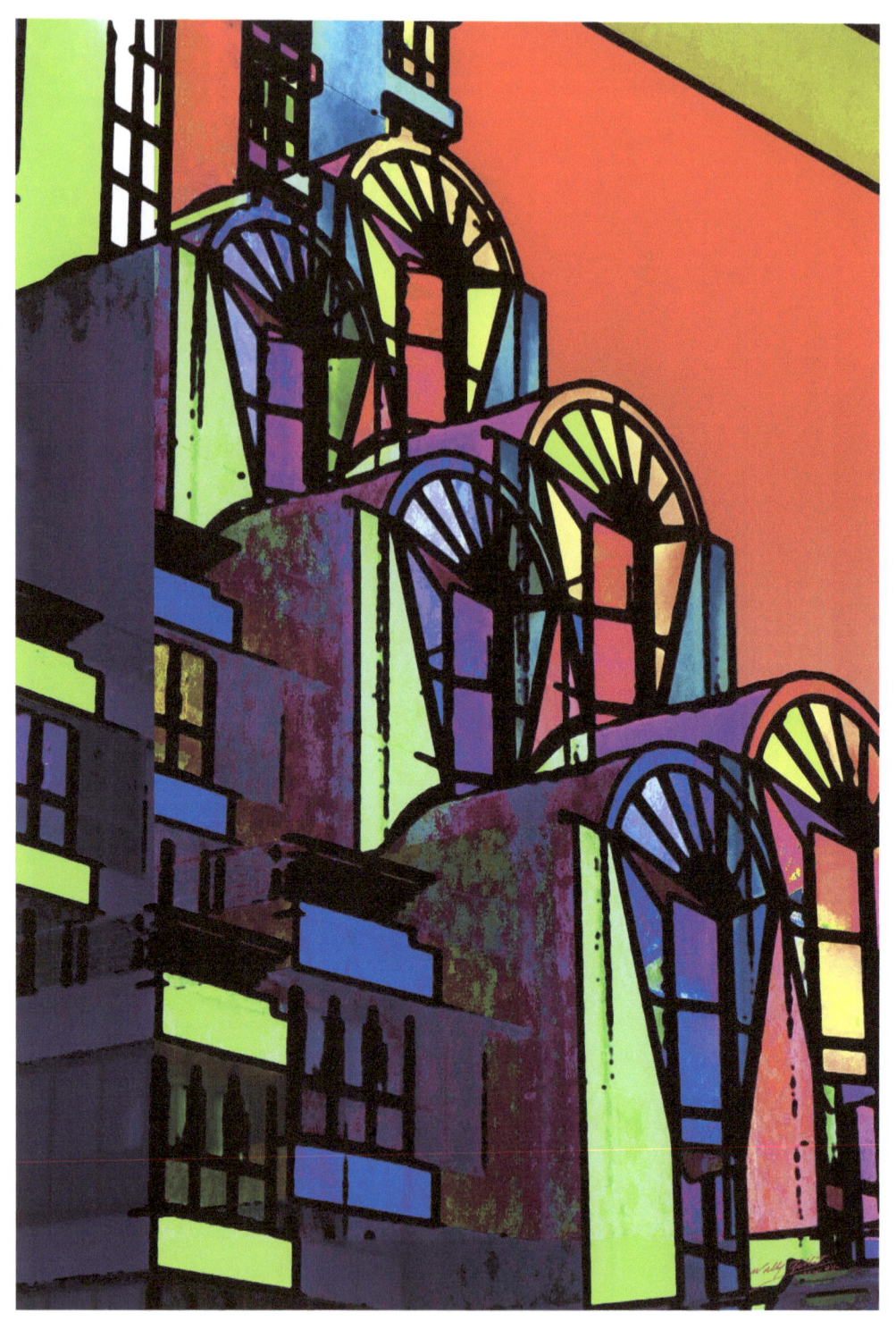

Fanlights – Red

2018, 60" x 40",
Printed on Aluminum, edition of 5

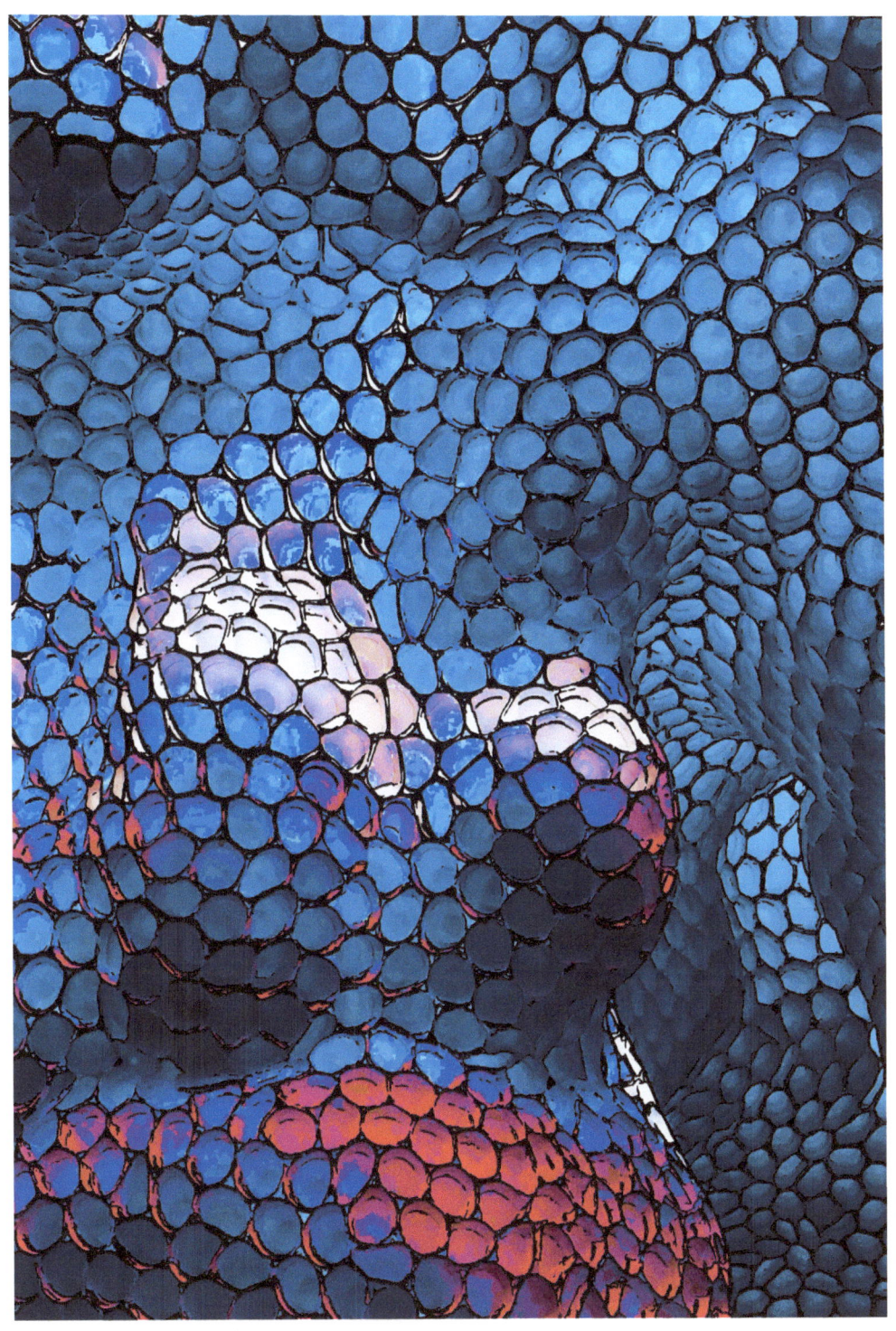

Swirls – Light Blue

2018, 36" x 24"
Printed on Aluminum, edition of 5

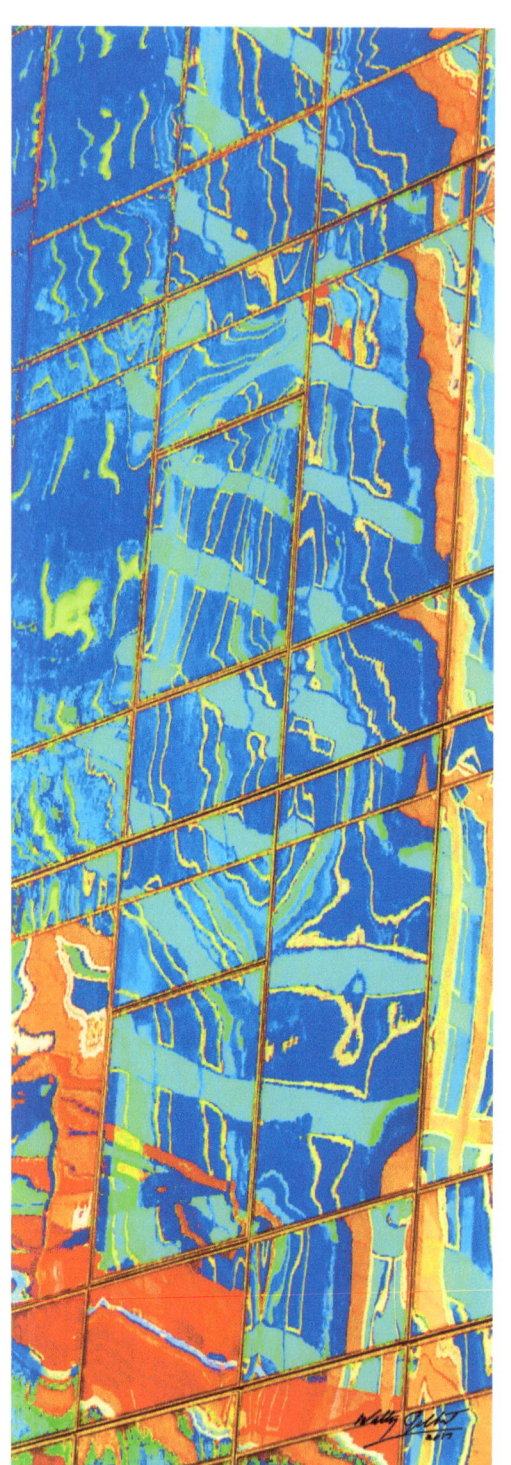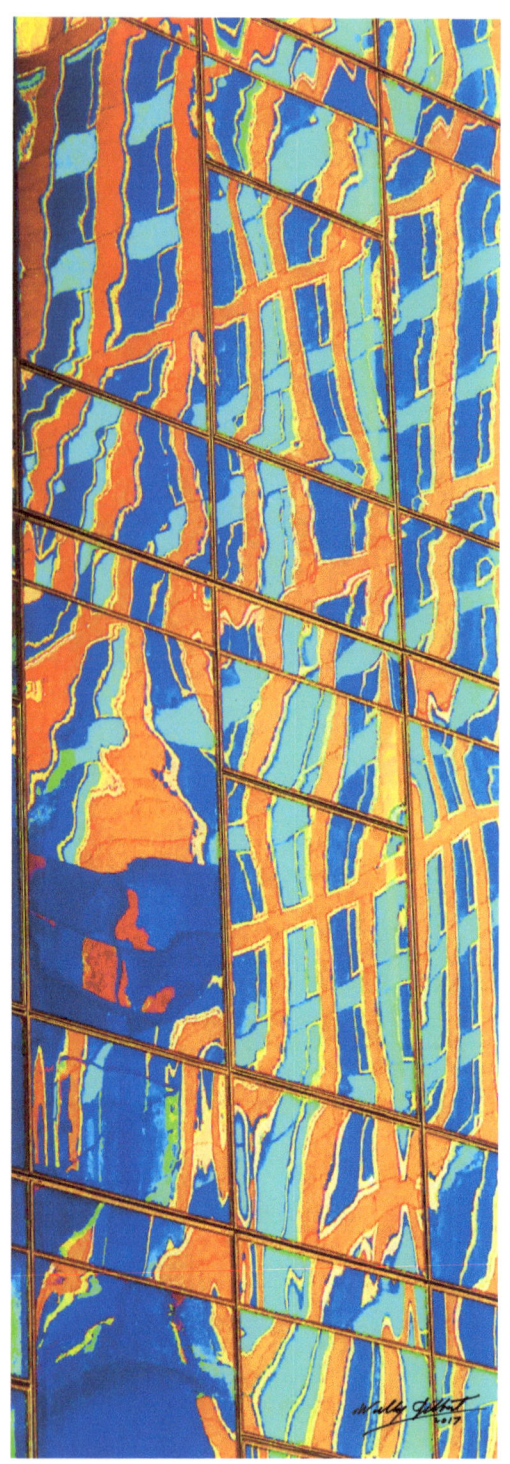

Windows Diptych #1

2017, Two Panels, each 36" x 12",
Printed on Aluminum, edition of 5

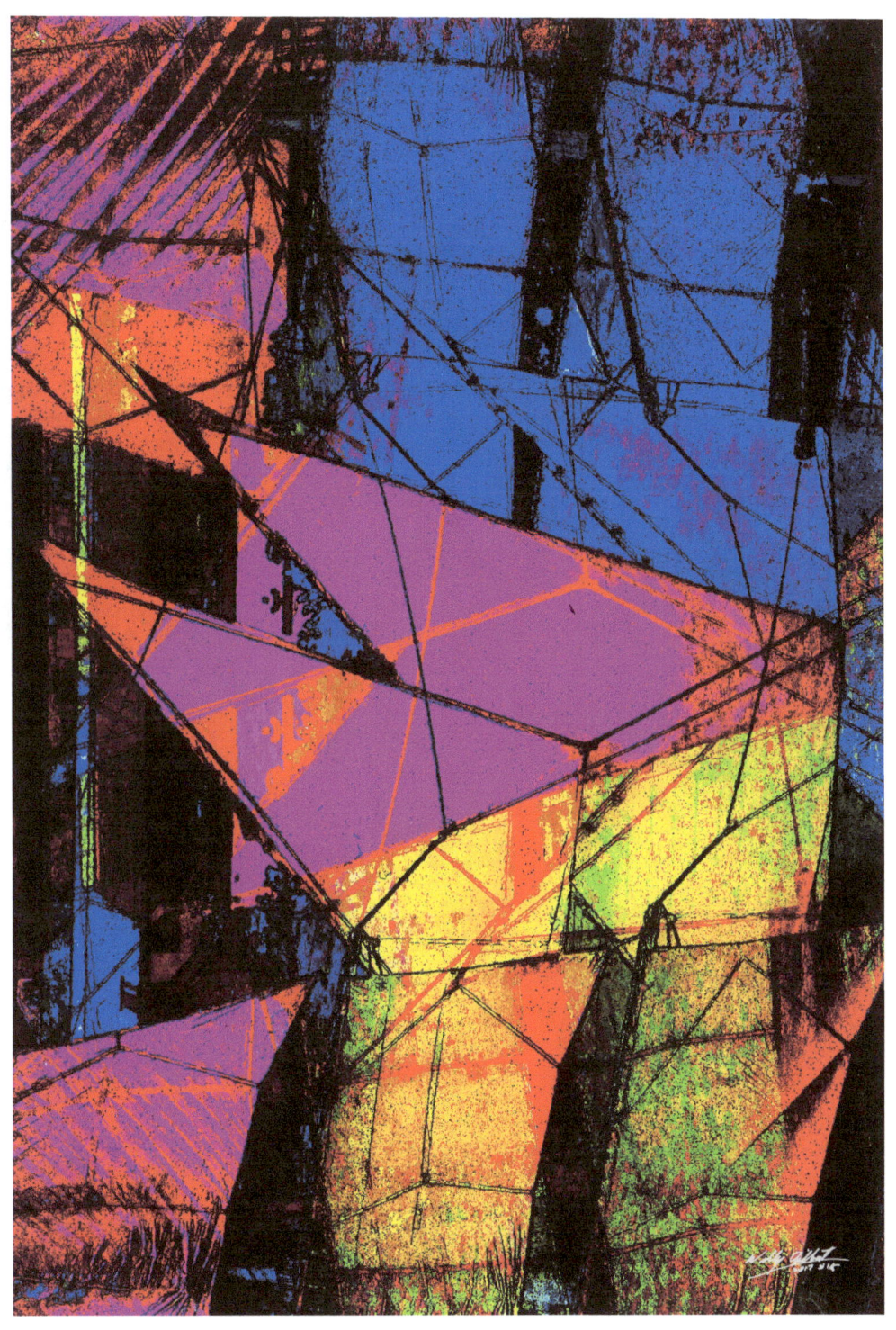

Torment

2017, 36" x 24",
Printed on Aluminum, edition of 5

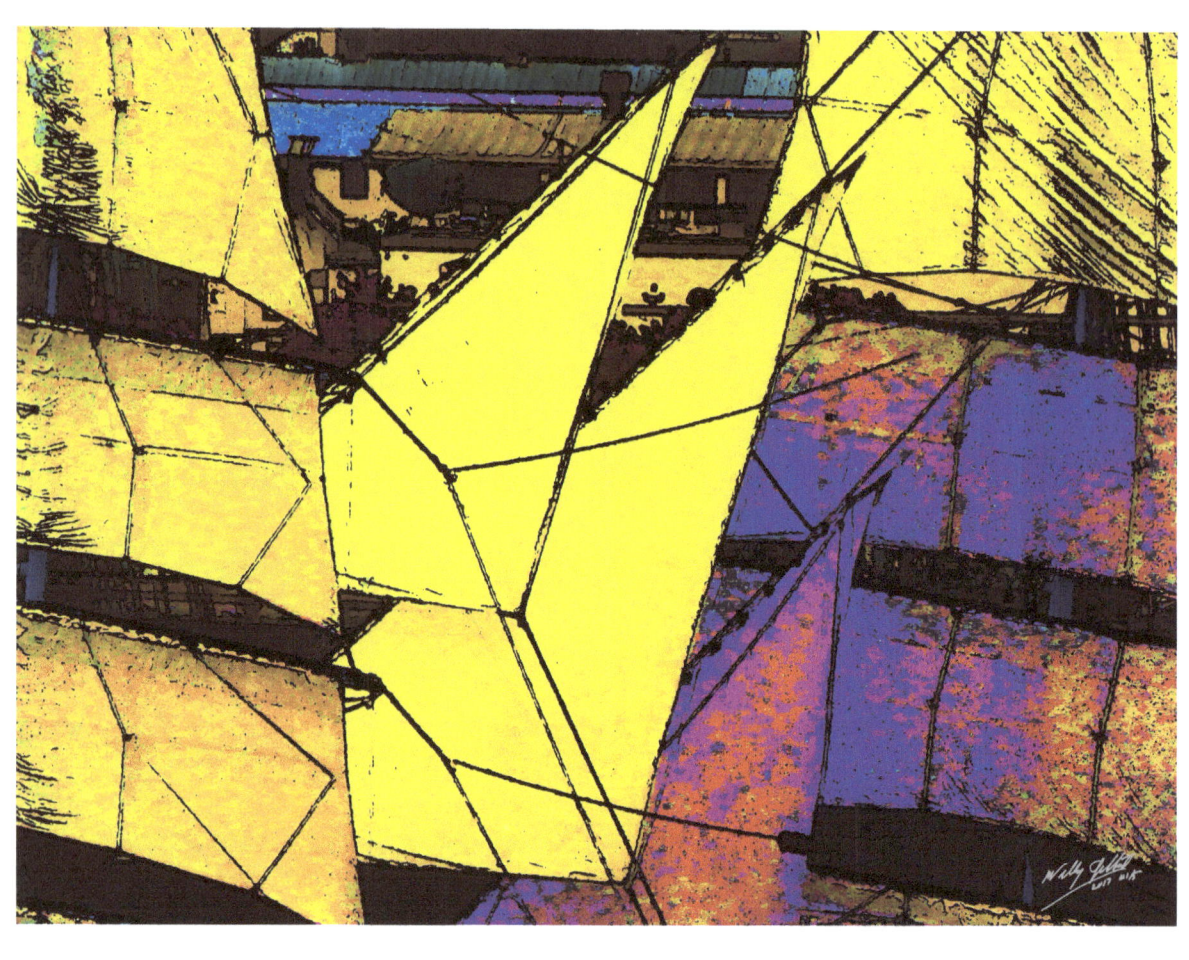

Sails #2 - Yellow

2017, 24" x 36",
Printed on Aluminum, edition of 5

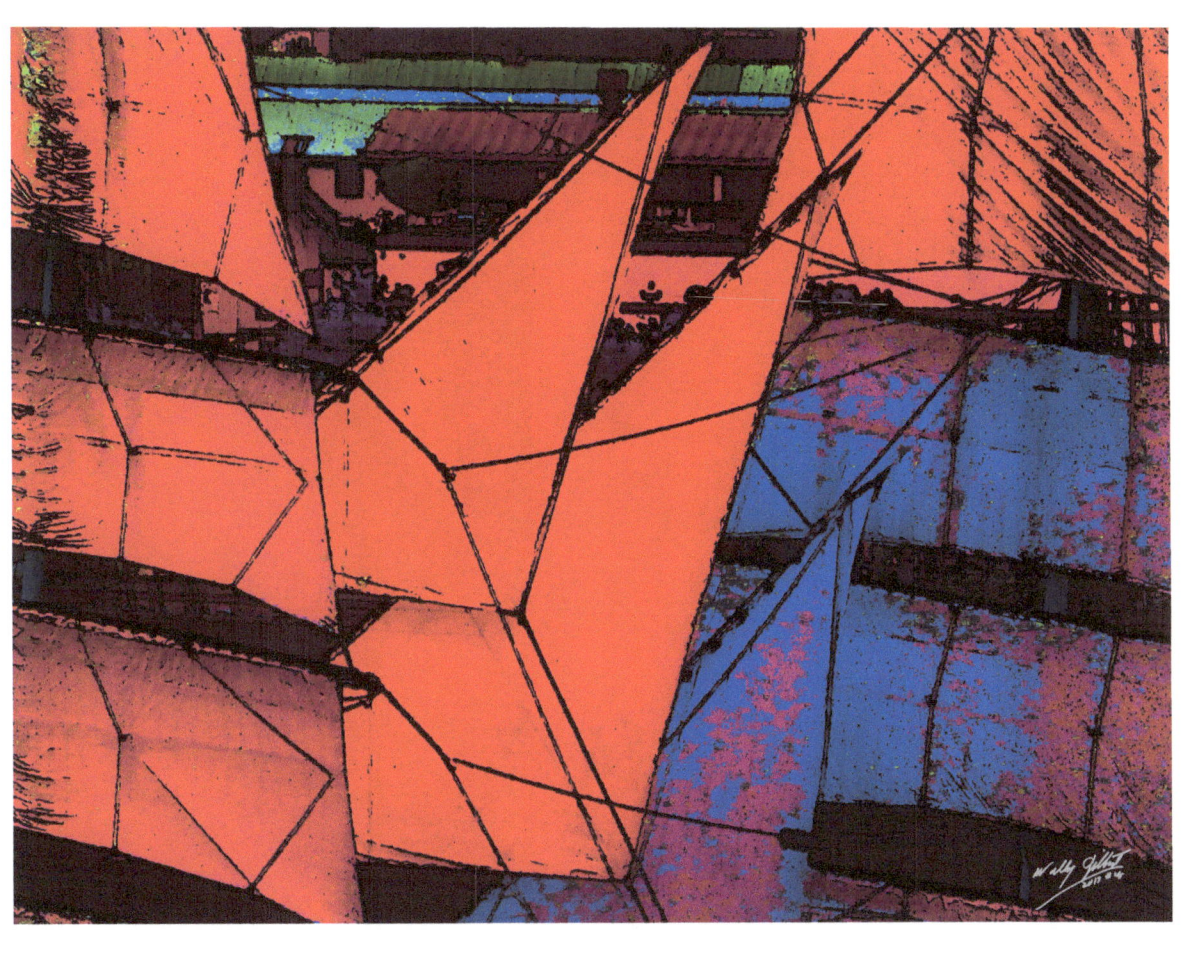

Sails #2 - Red

2017, 24" x 36",
Printed on Aluminum, edition of 5

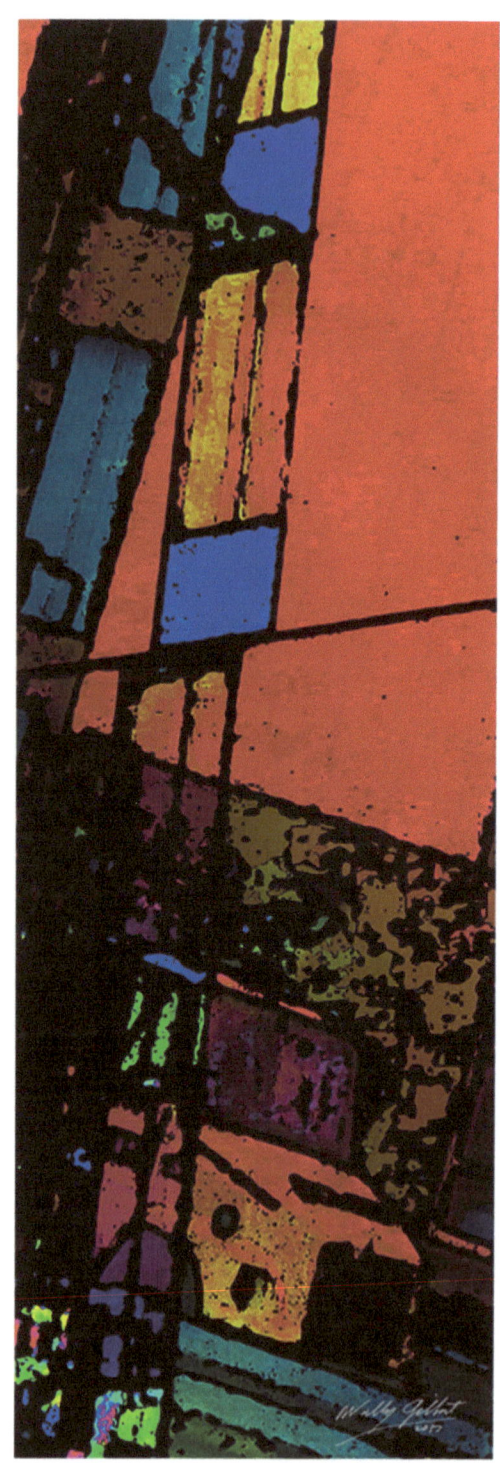 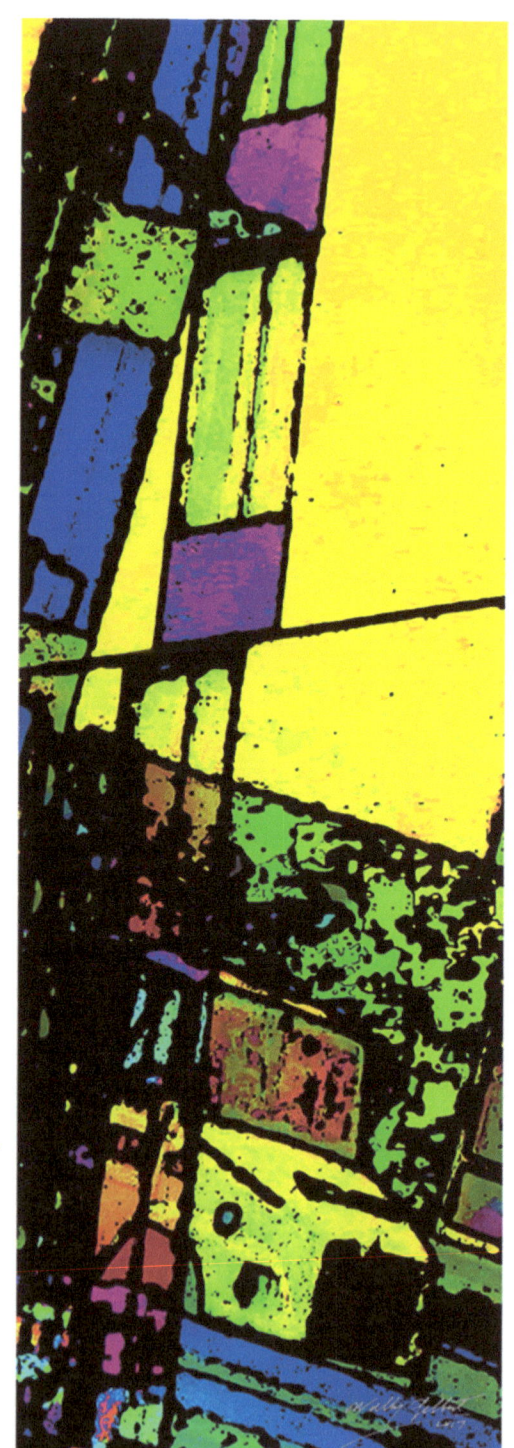

Old Car Diptych

2016, Two Panels, each 36" x 12",
Printed on Aluminum, edition of 5

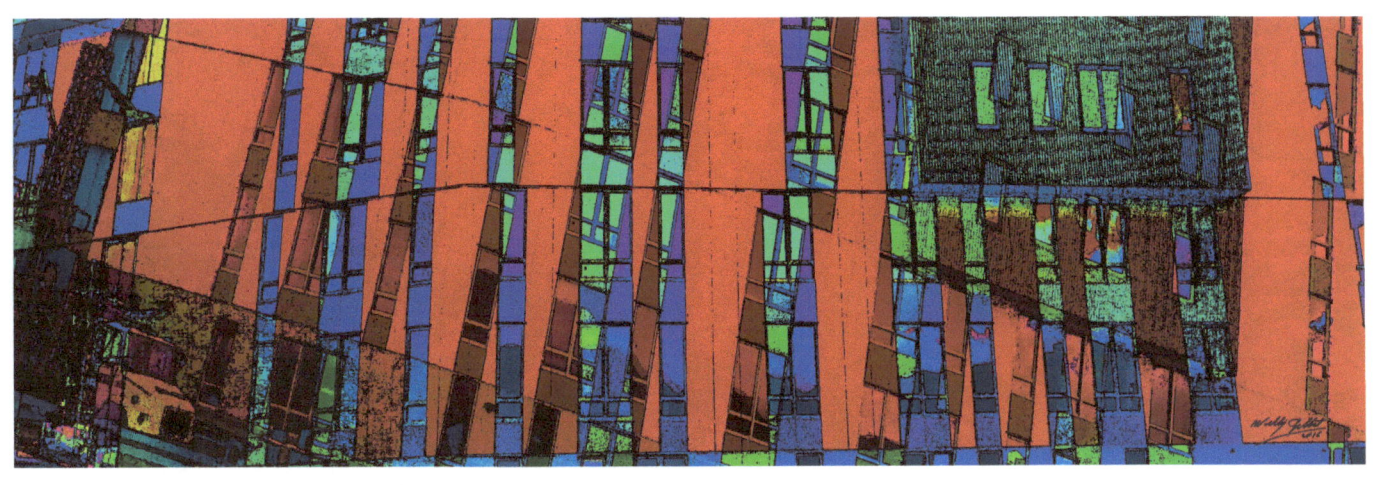

Torn Building #2 – Red

2016 20" X 60",
Printed on Aluminum, edition of 5

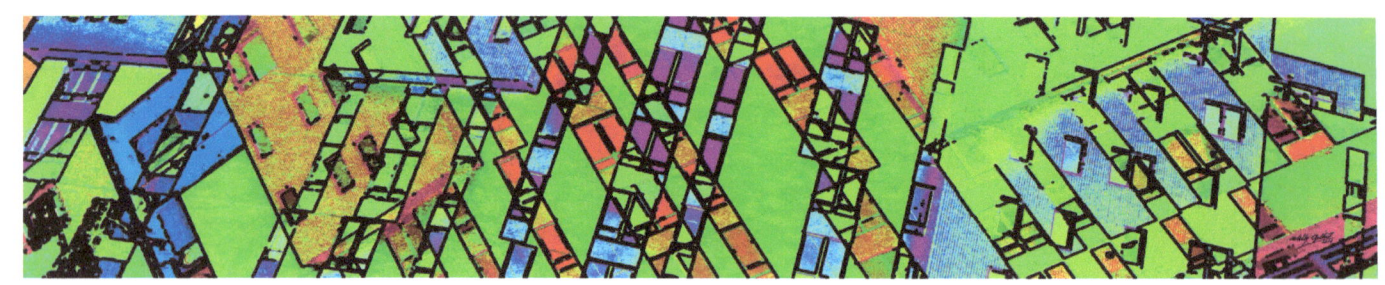

Torn Building – Green

2016, 14" x 72",
Printed on Aluminum, edition of 5

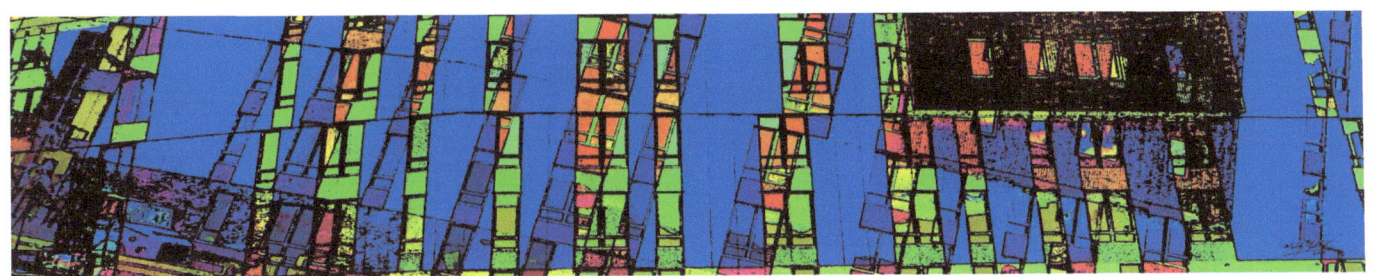

Torn Building #2 – Blue

2016, 14" x 72",
Printed on Aluminum, edition of 5

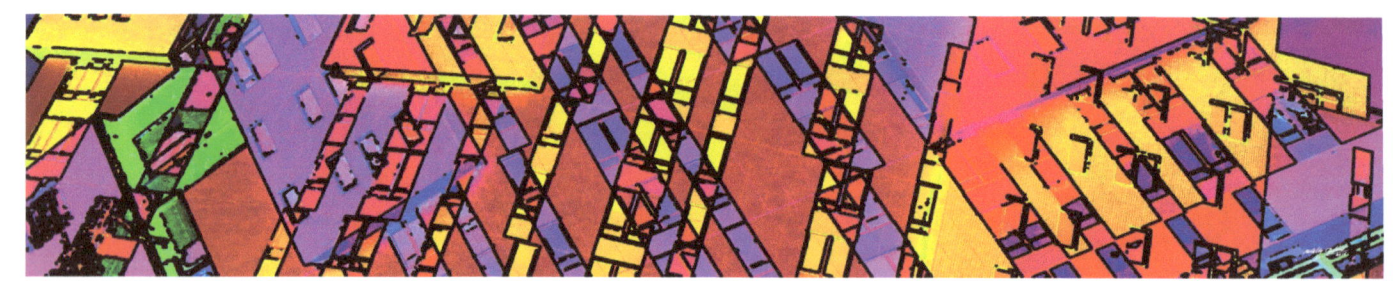

Torn Building – Bright Red

2016, 14" x 72",
Printed on Aluminum, edition of 5

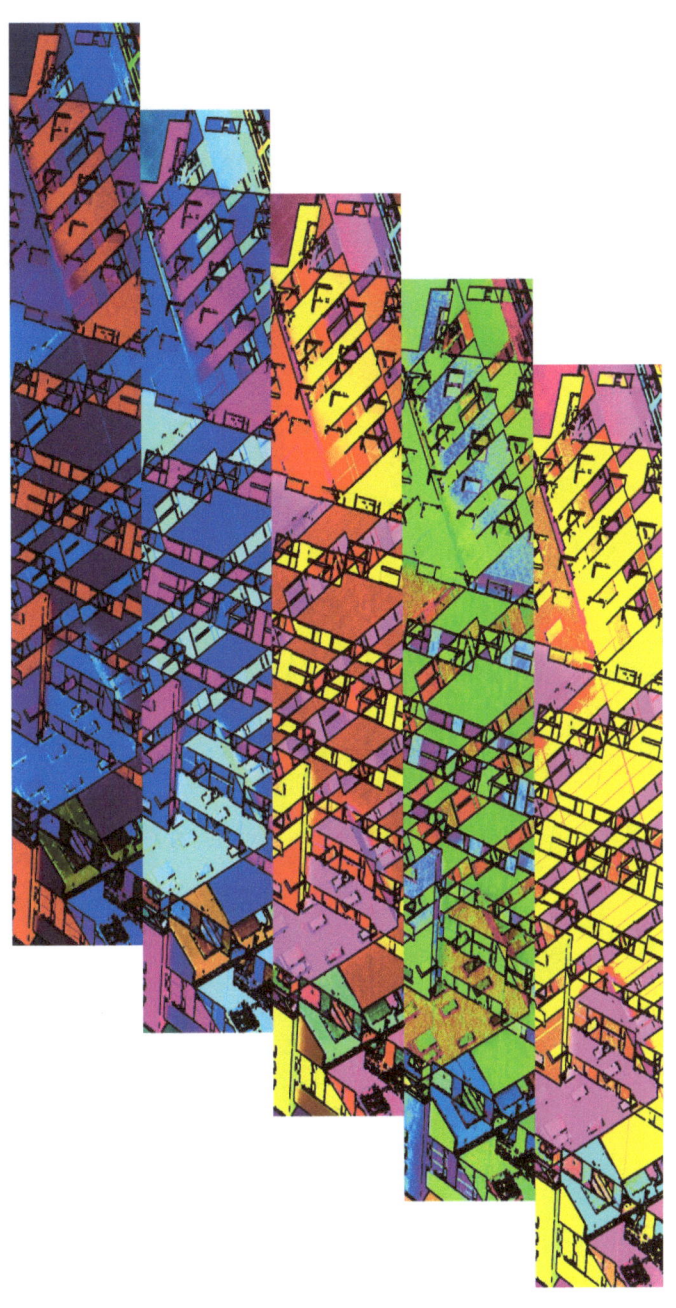

Torn Building Towers

2016, Five Panels, each 72" x 10",
Printed on Aluminum, edition of 5.

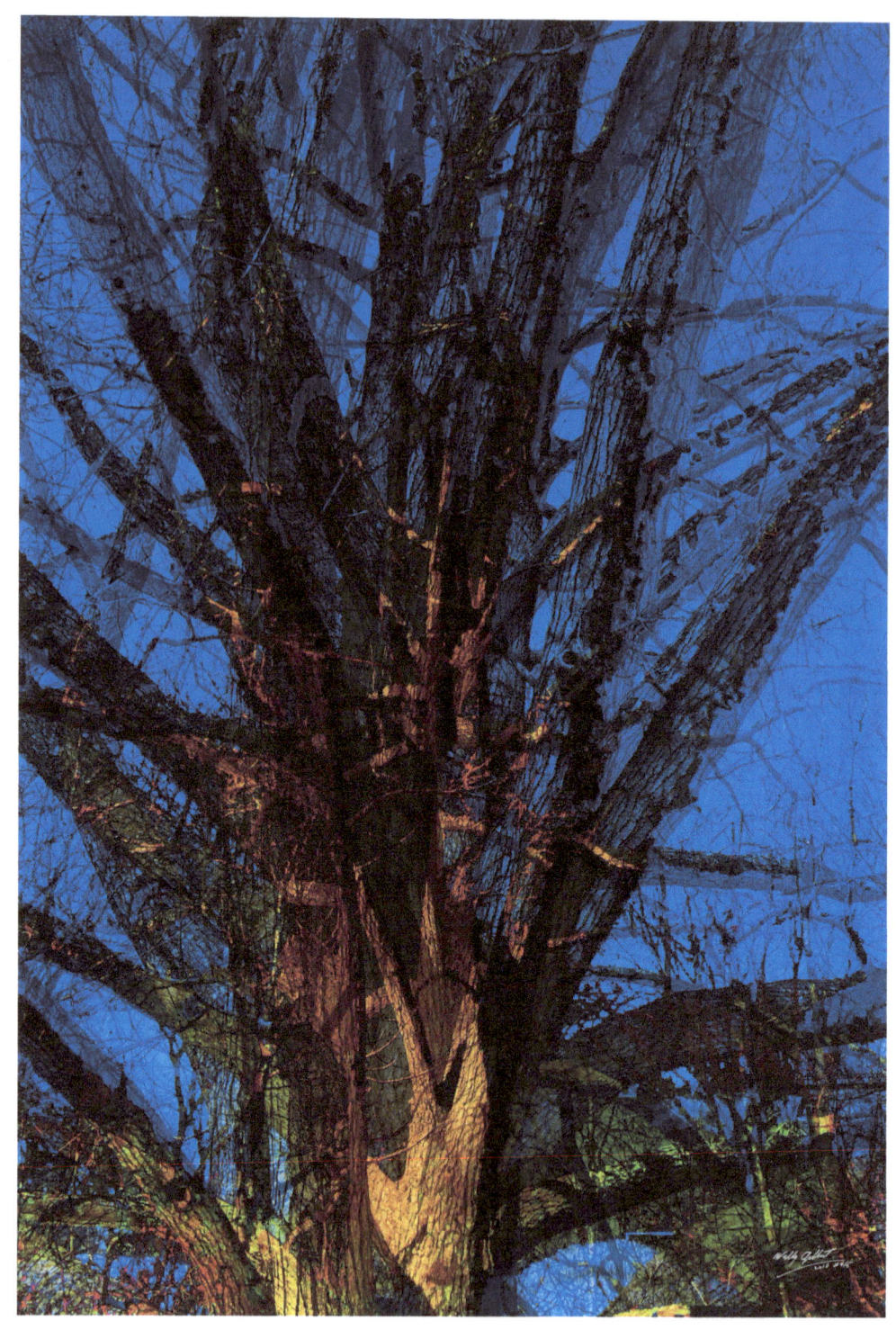

Trees – Blue

2015, 60" x 40",
Printed on A4uminum, edition of 5

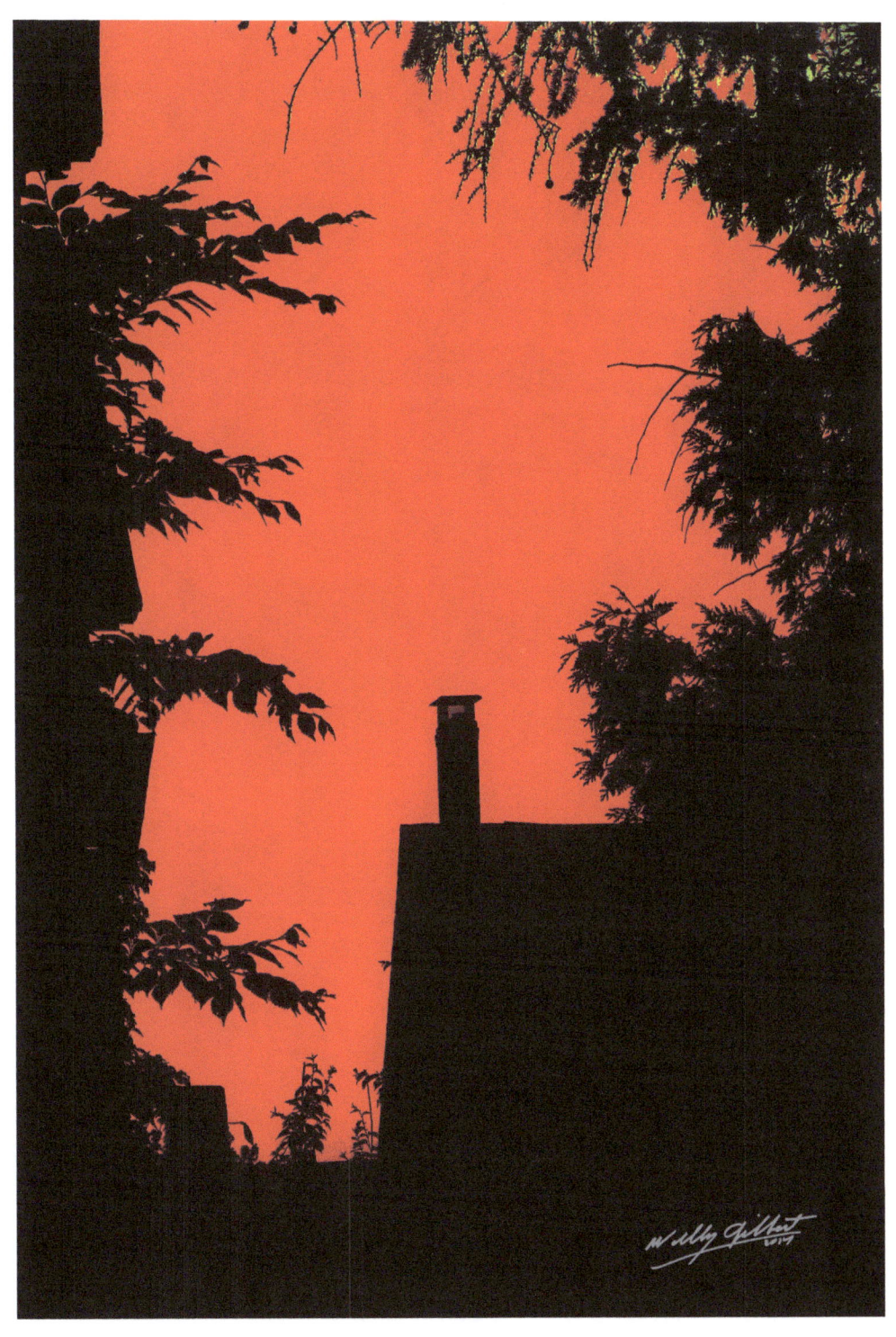

Red Sky #2

2014, 36" x 24",
Printed on Aluminum, edition of 5

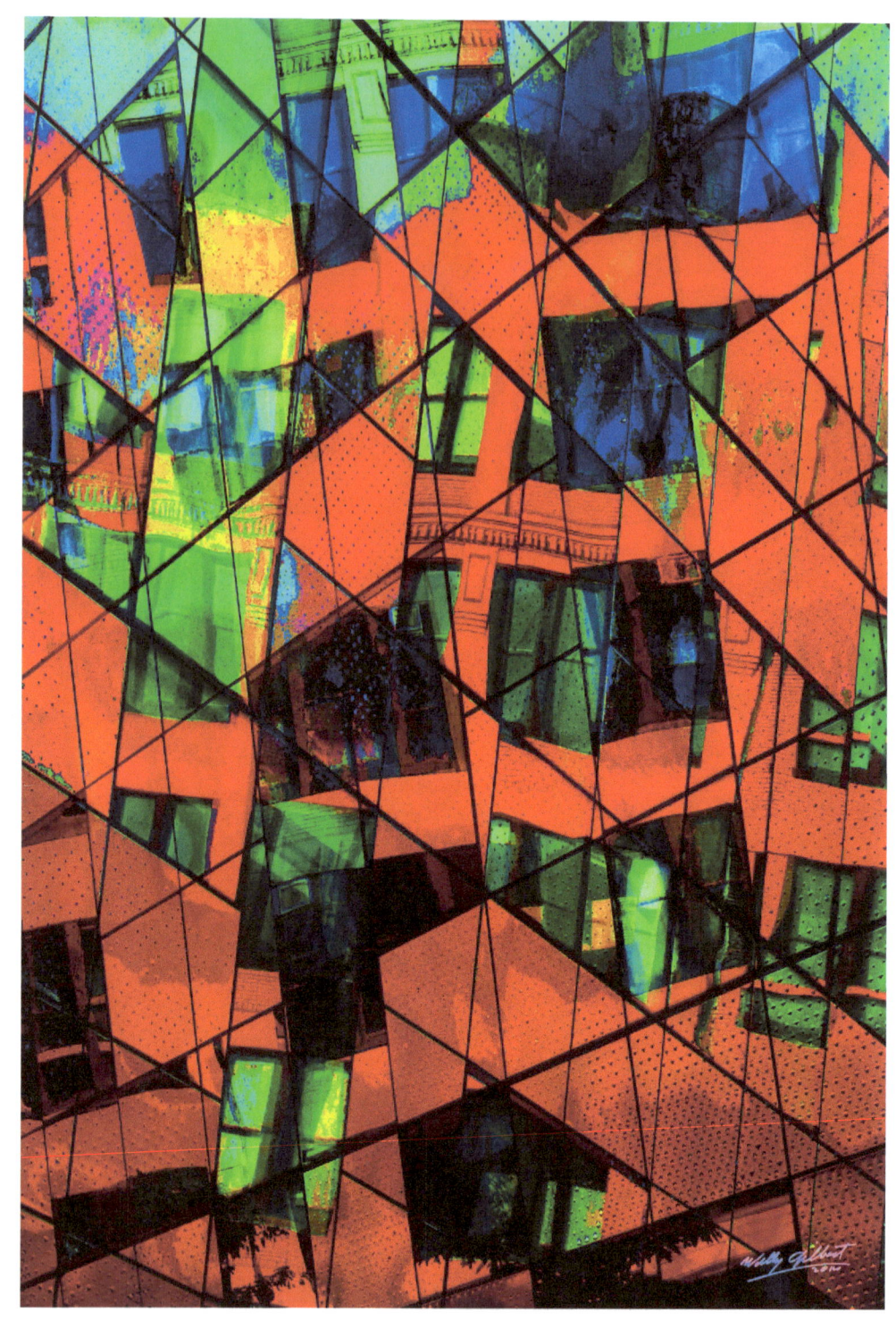

Broken City

2014, 36" x 24",
Printed on Aluminum, edition of 5

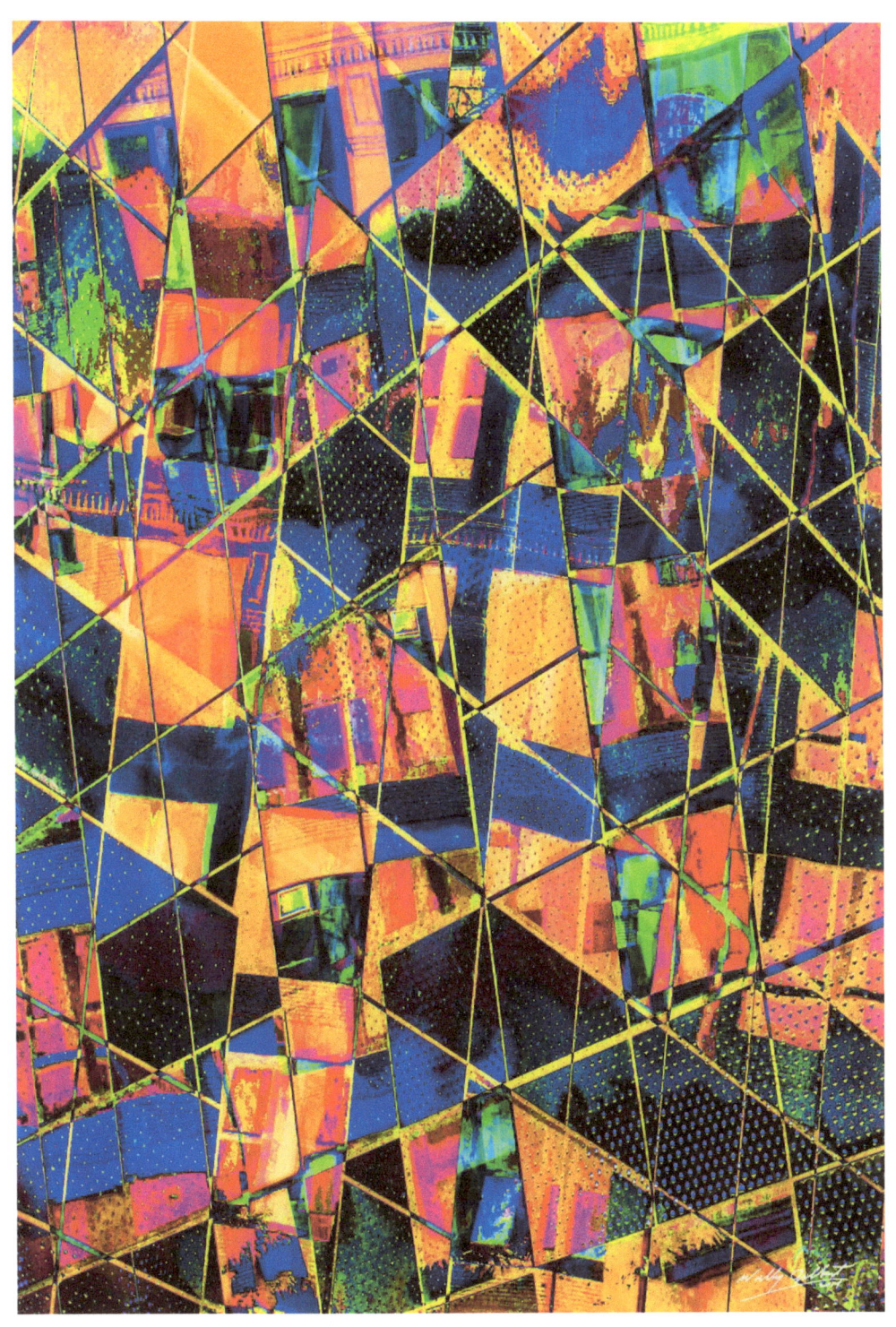

Broken City #II

2014, 36" x 24",
Printed on Aluminum, edition of 5

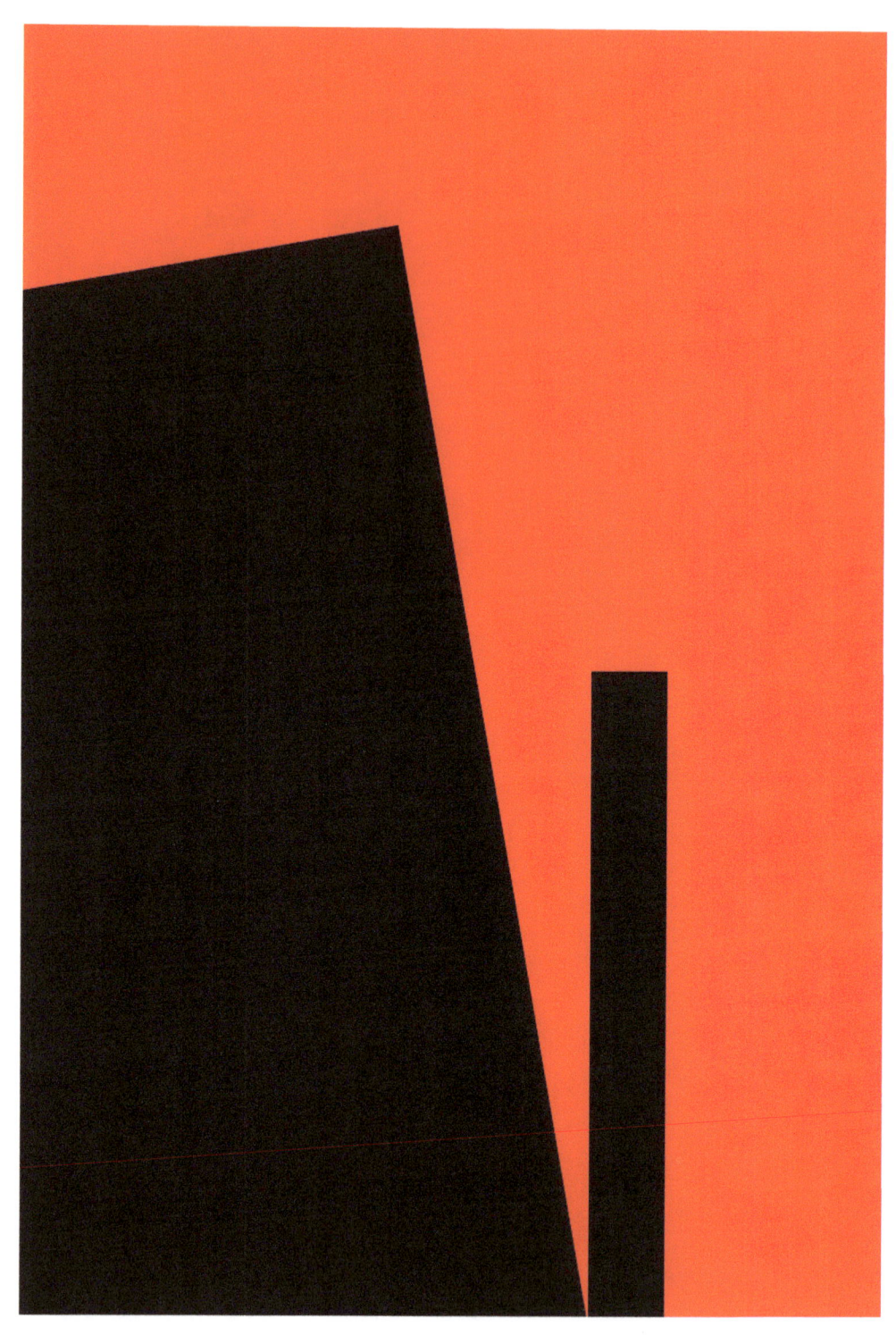

Black on Red #5

2014, 36" x 24"
C-Print Face-Mounted on Plexiglas, Edition of 3
From the Forms Series

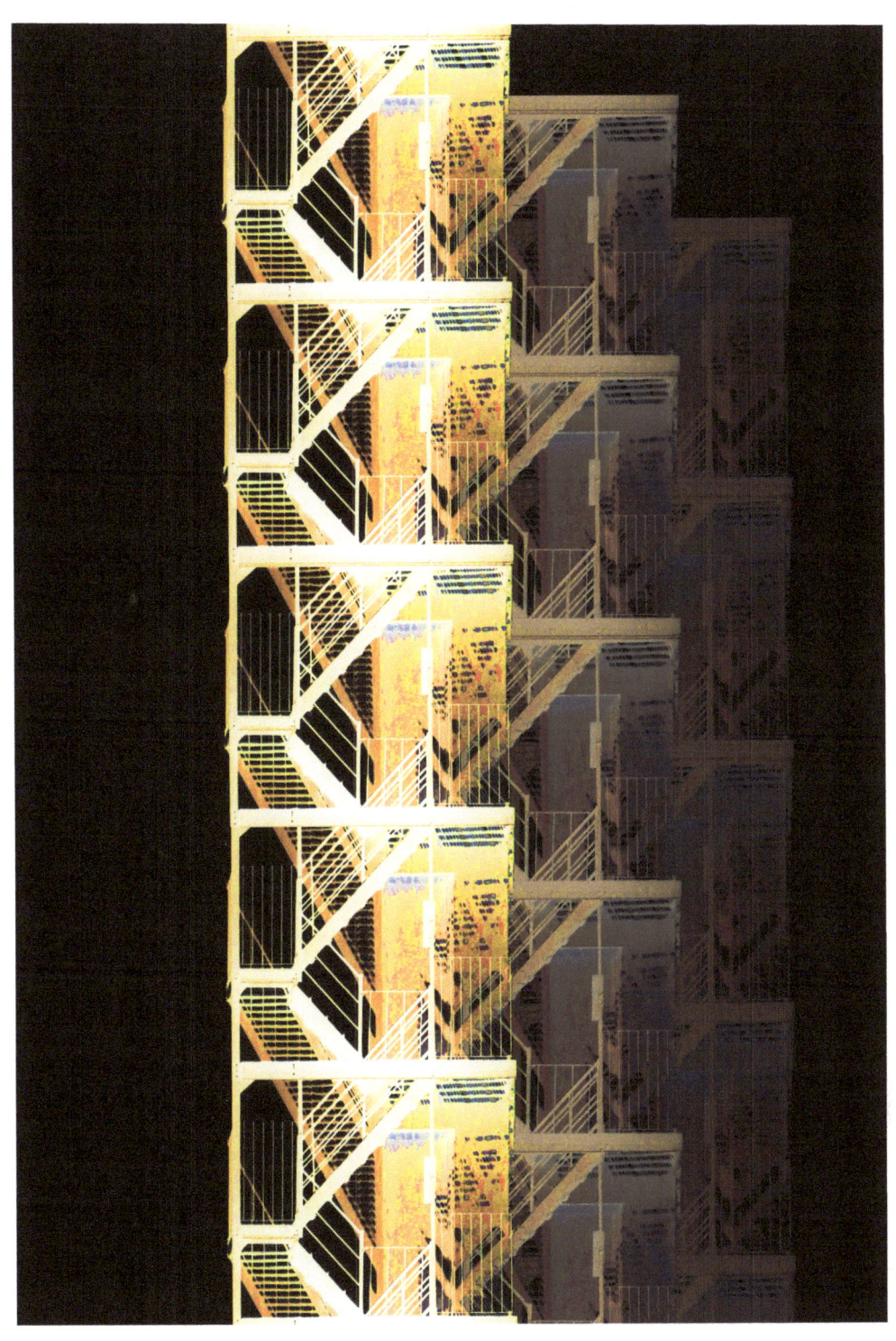

Jacob's Ladder

2014, 36" x 24"
Printed on Aluminum, edition of 5

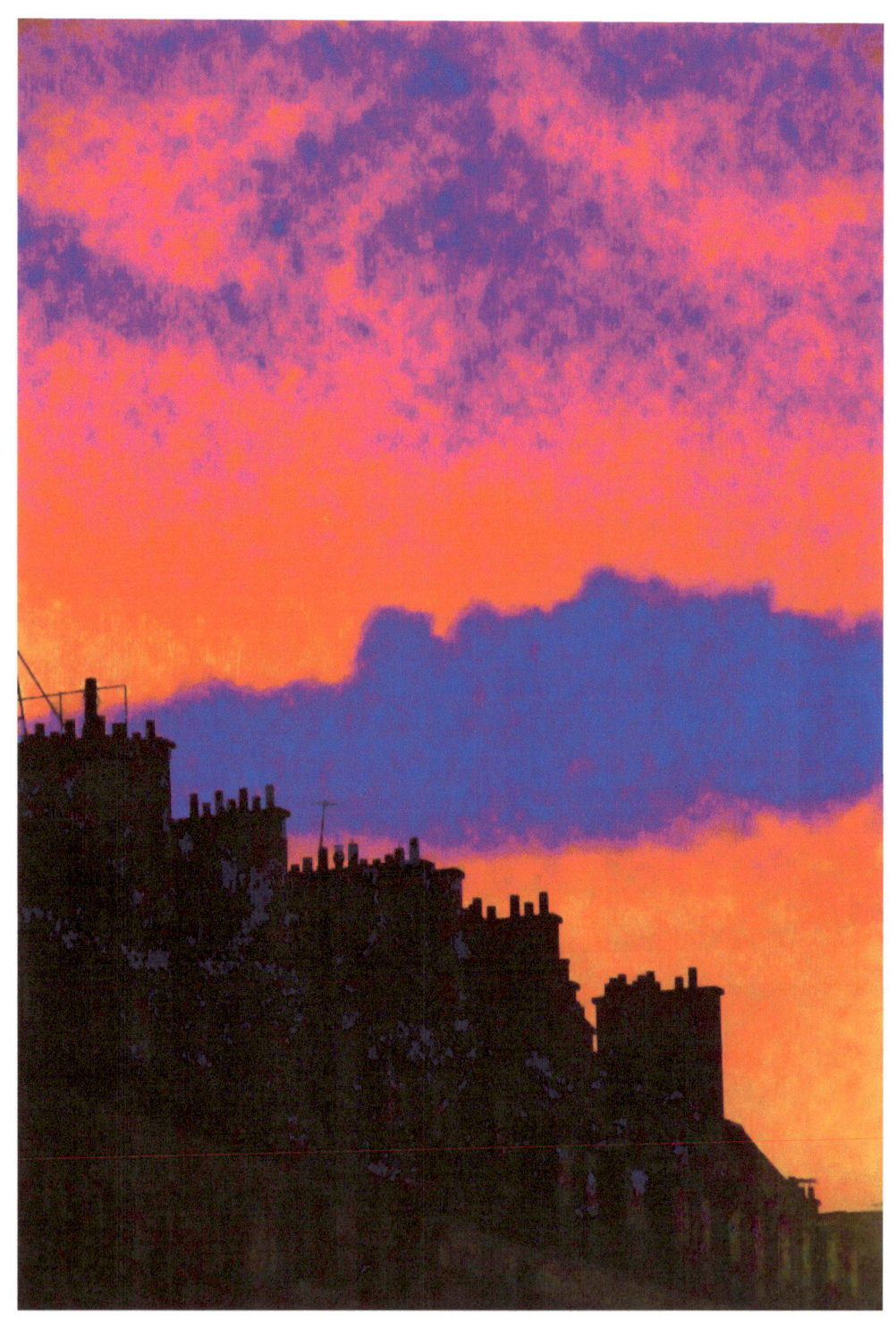

Dawn – Paris

2011, 36" x 24"
C-Print Face-Mounted on Plexiglas, Edition of 3

Bands #10ab

2011, 36" x 24"
C-Print Face-Mounte1d on Plexiglas, Edition of 3
From the Lines Series

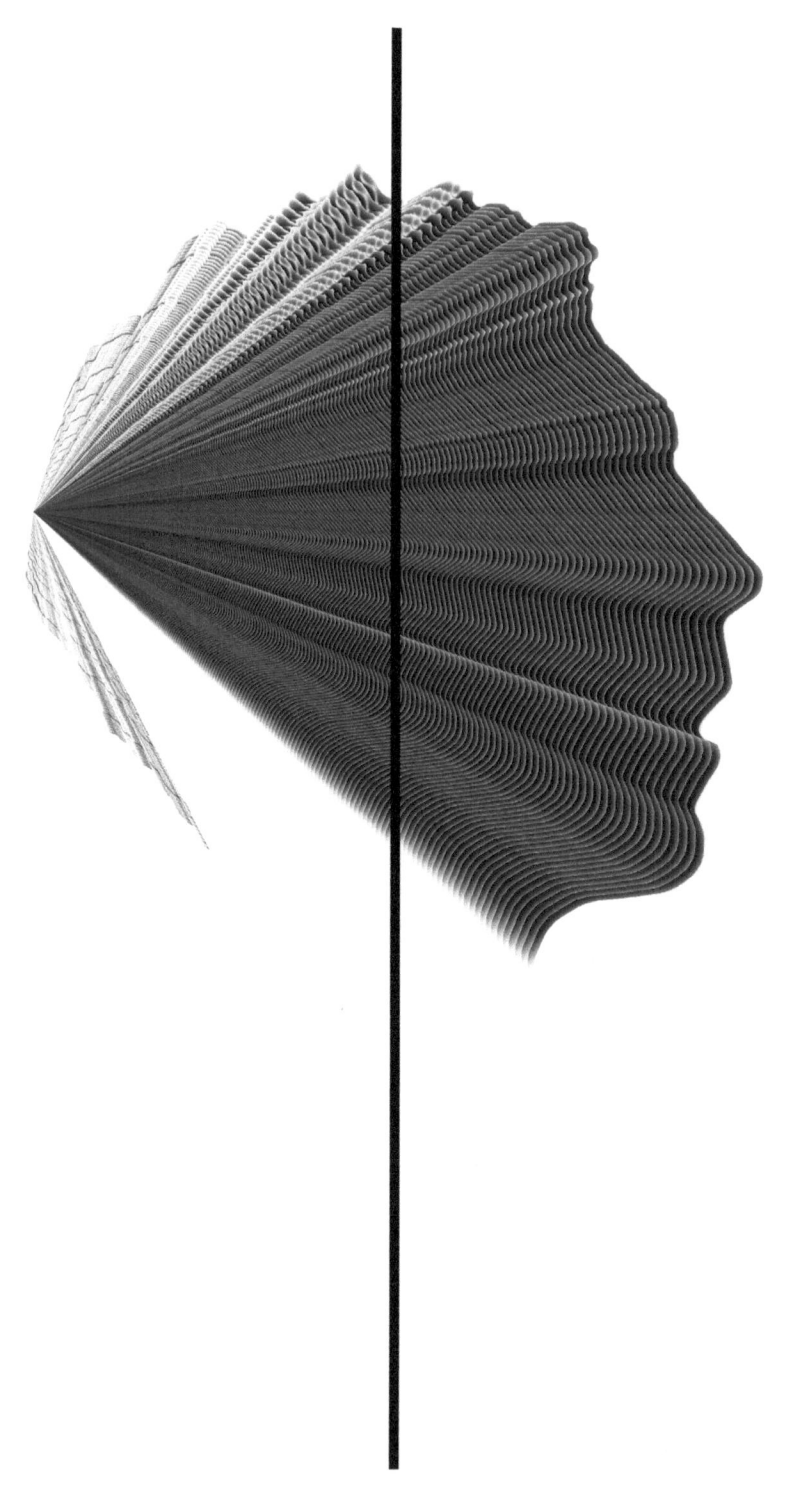

Vanishing #2 – Diptych

2009, 72" x 48",
Printed on Aluminum, edition of 5

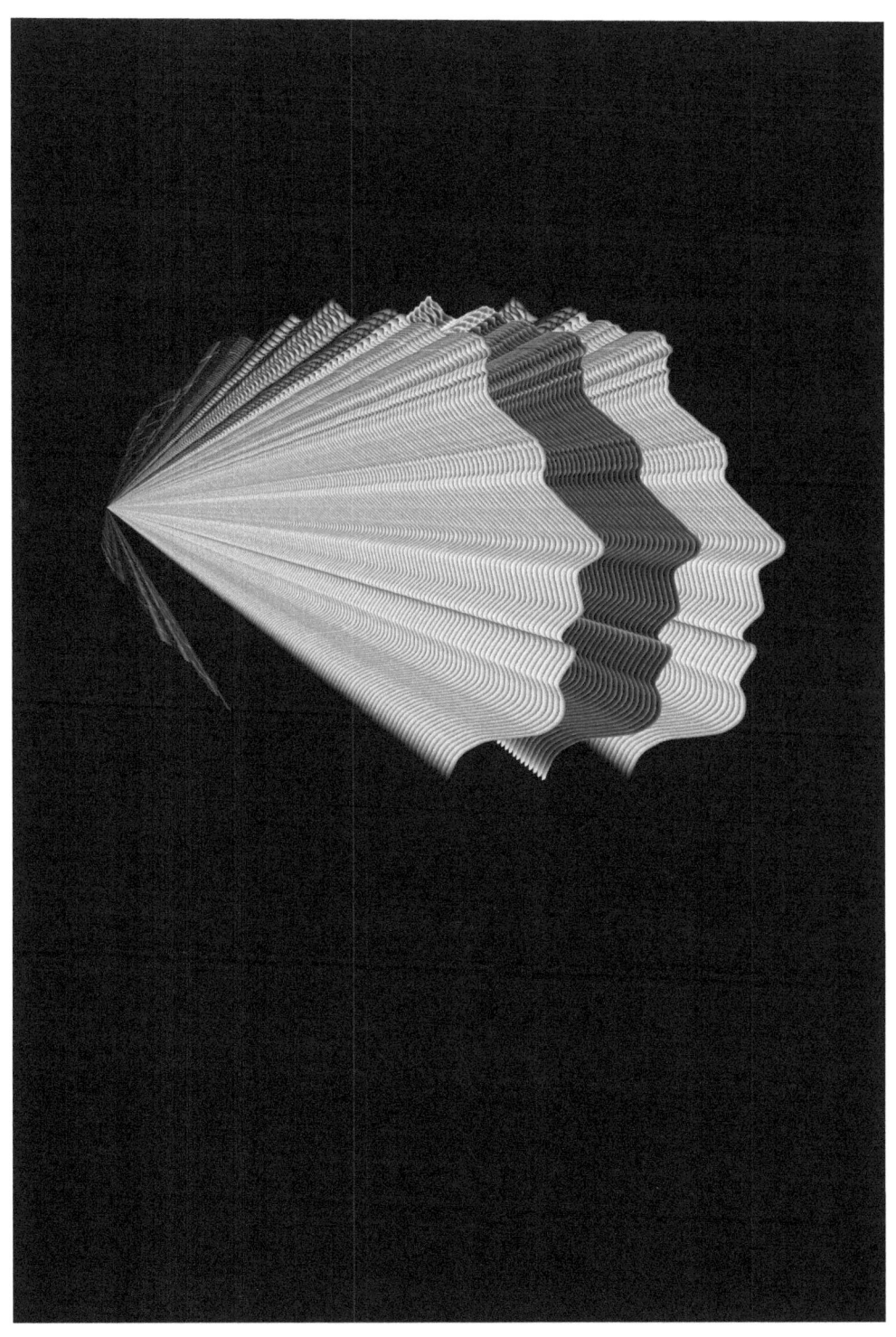

Three Heads

2009, 36"x 24"
C-Prints Face-Mounted on Plexiglas, Edition of 3
From the Vanishing Series

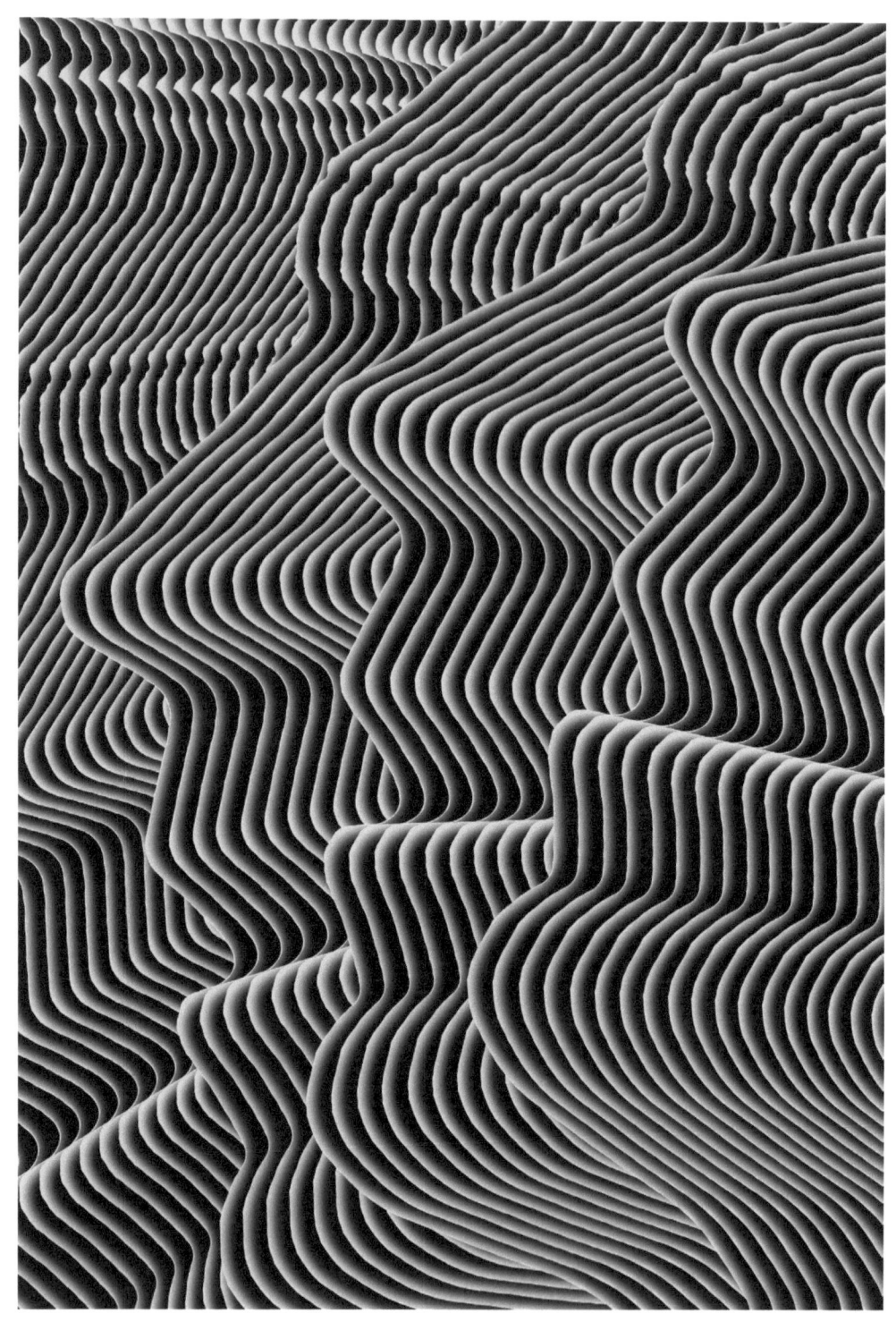

Four Faces

2009, 36" x 24"
C-Print Face-Mounted on Plexiglas, Edition of 3
From the Vanishing Series

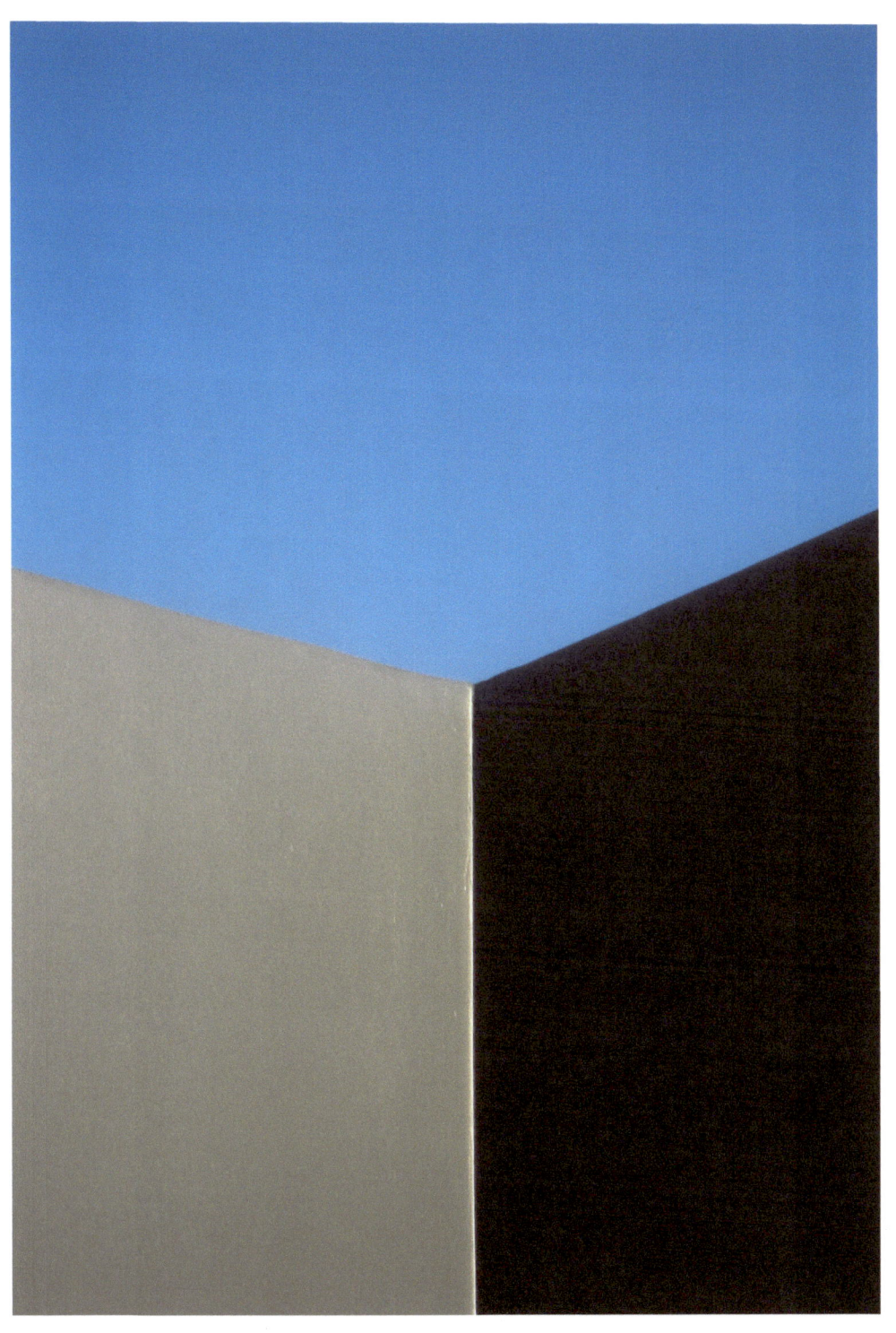

Corner – Los Angeles

2007, 36" x 24"
C-Print Face-Mounted on Plexiglas, Edition of 3

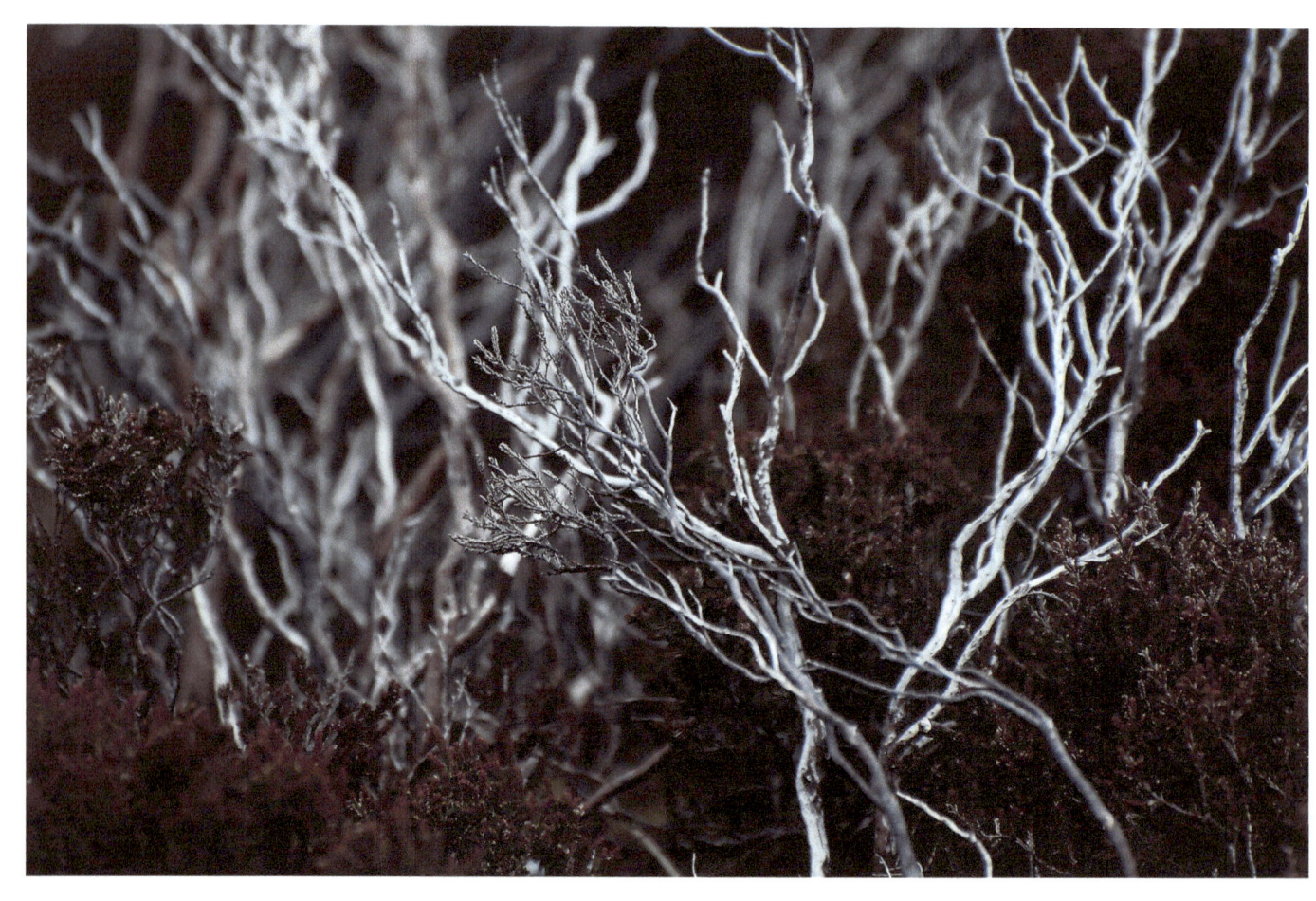

Where The Wild Things Are #2 – Orkney

2007, 24" x 36"
C-Print Face-Mounted on Plexiglas, Edition of 3
From the Orkney Series

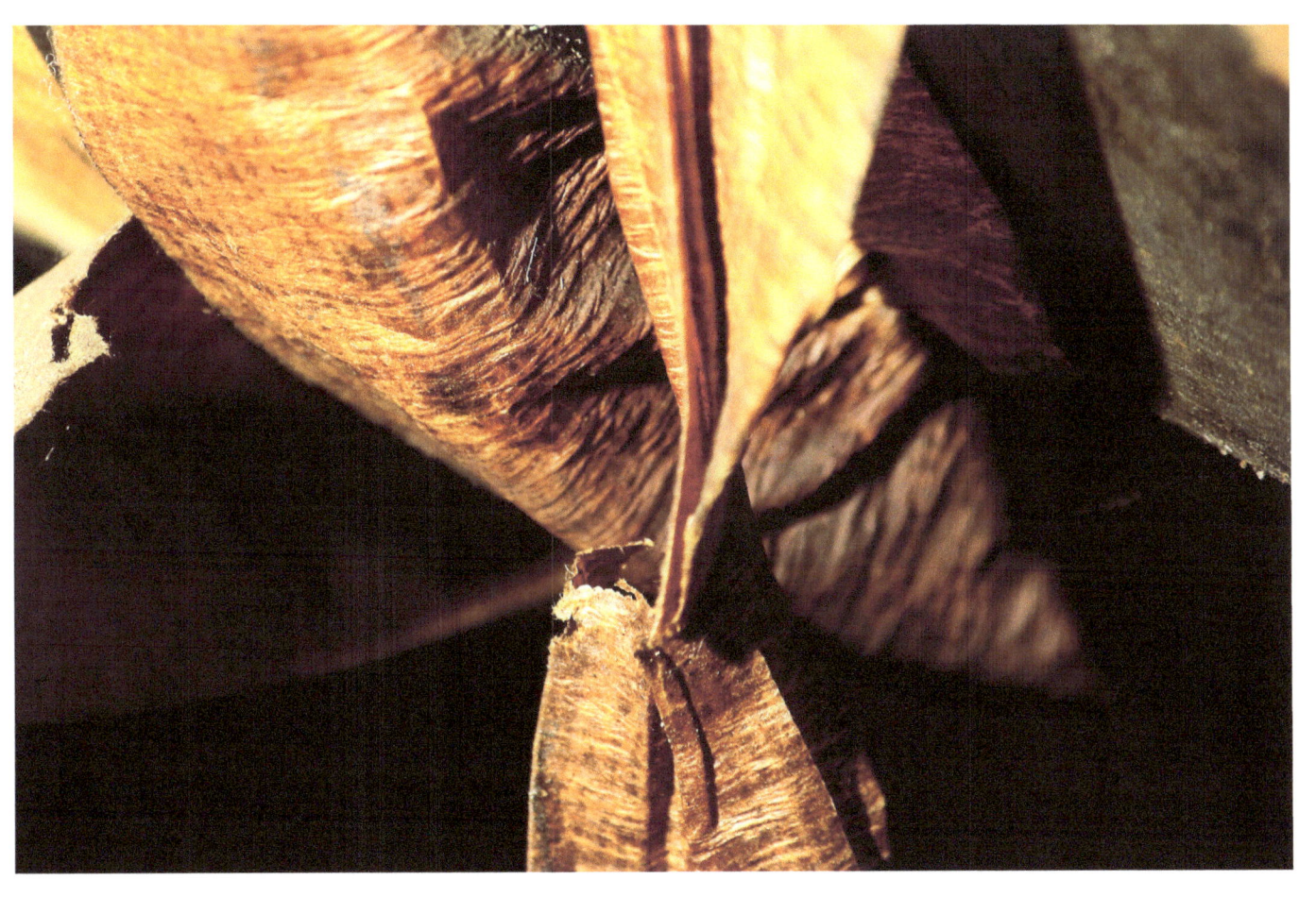

Paper #1 – Warsaw

2006, 24" x 36"
C-Print Face-Mounted on Plexiglas, Edition of 3
From the Norblin: Images of Decay Series

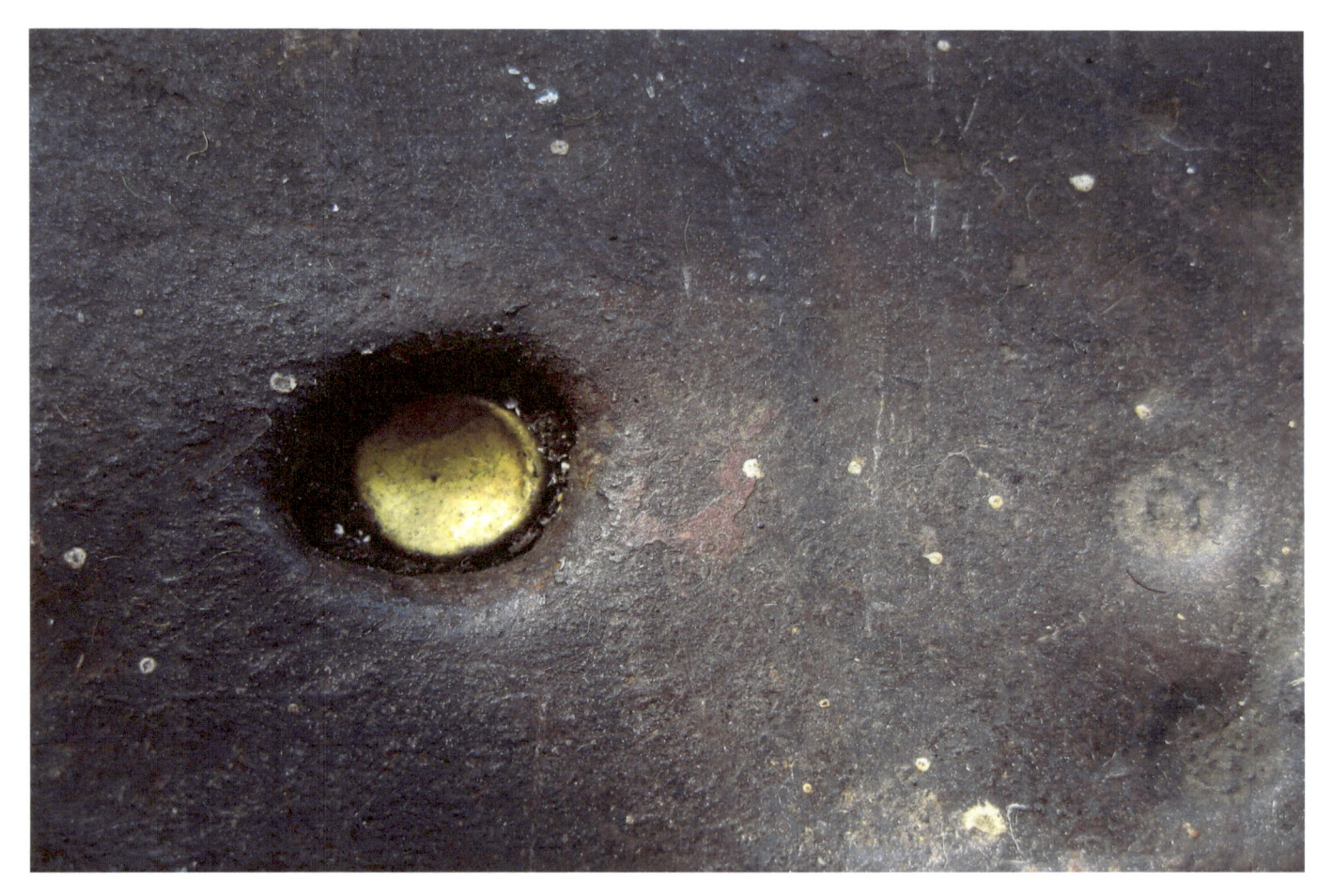

Rivet #1 – Warsaw

2006, 24" x 36"
C-Print Face-Mounted on Plexiglas, Edition of 3
From the Norblin: Images of Decay Series

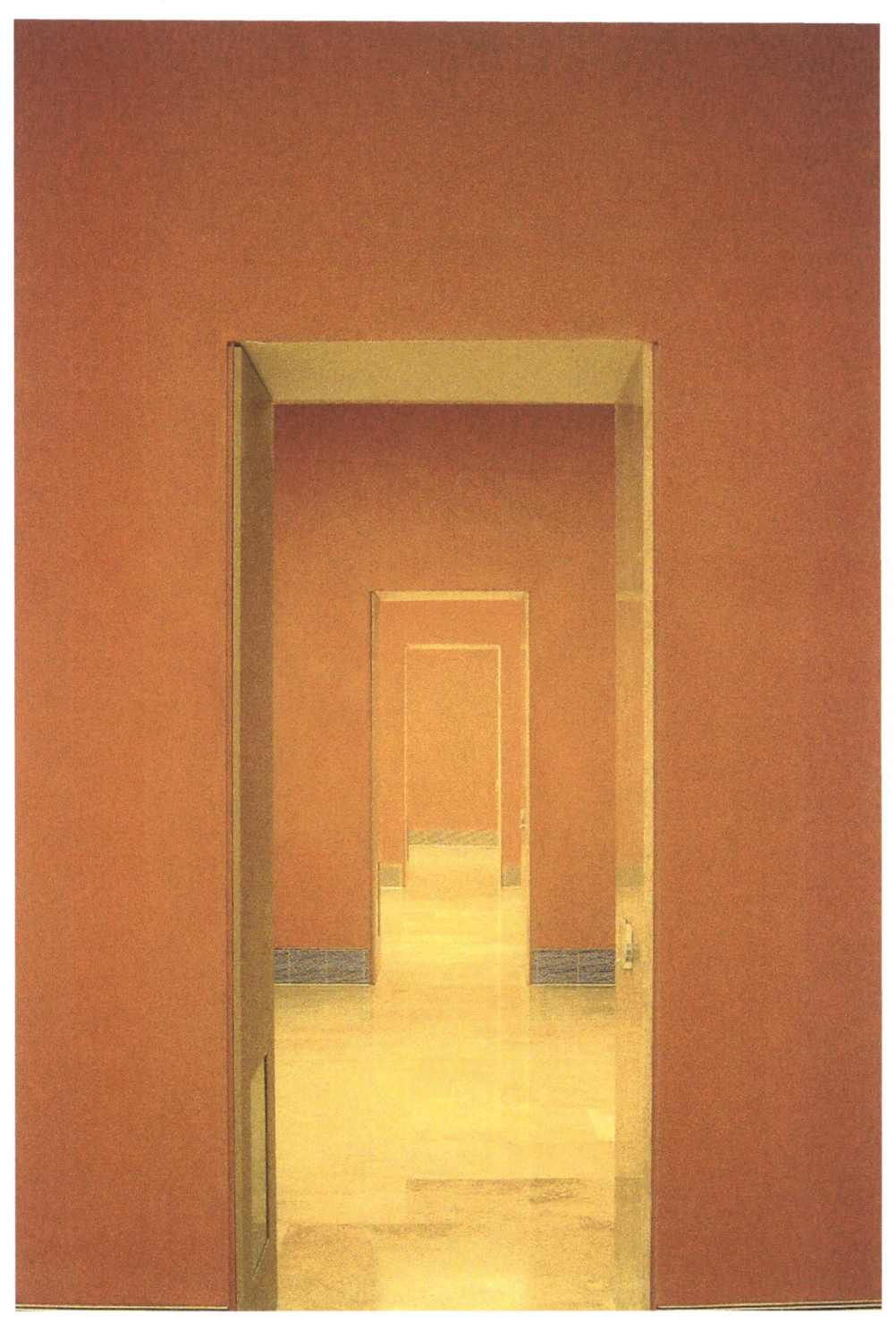

Three Doors – Madrid

2004, 72" x 48",
C-print on Ultraboard, edition of 5

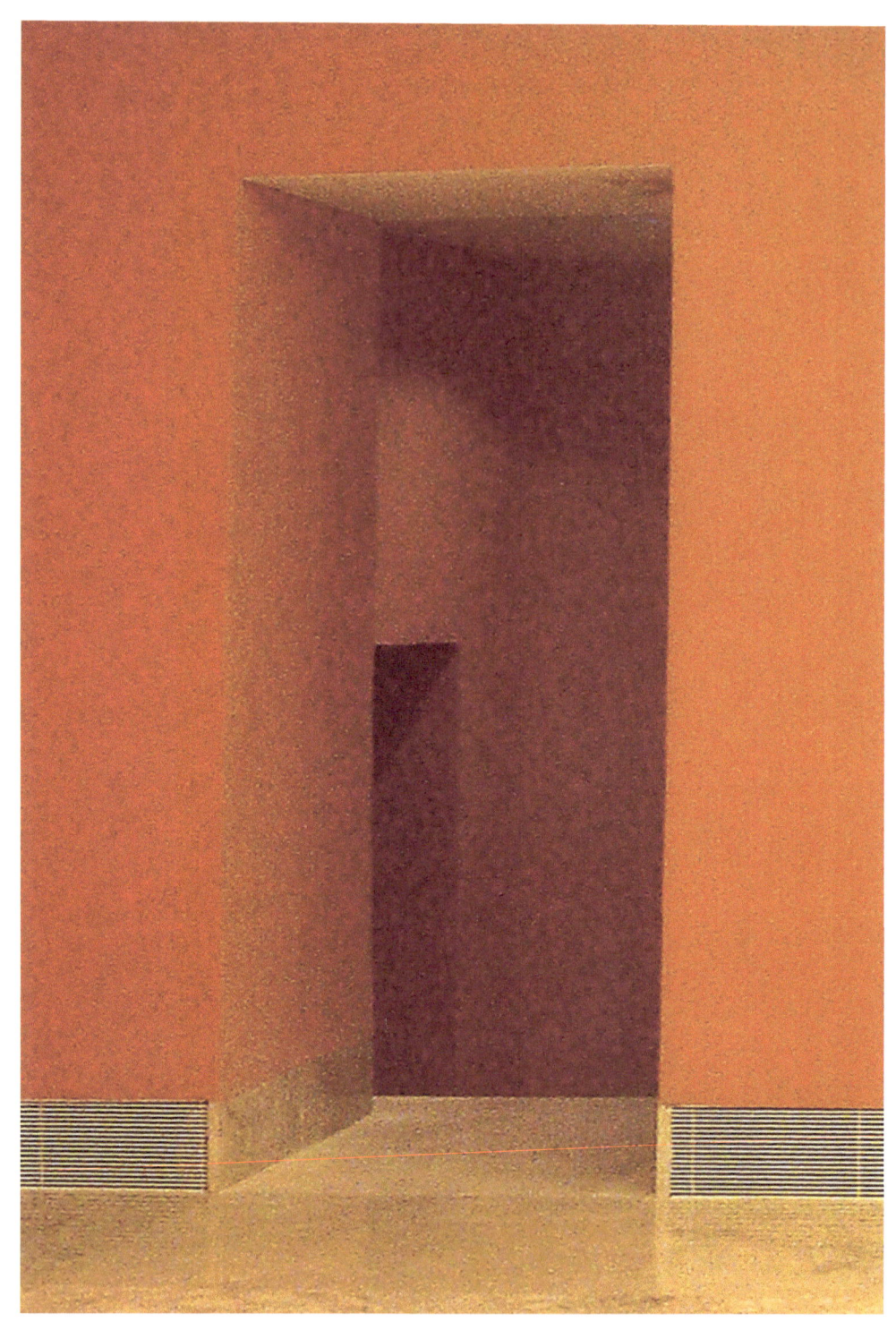

Door – Madrid

2004, 72" x 48",
C-print on Ultraboard, edition of 5

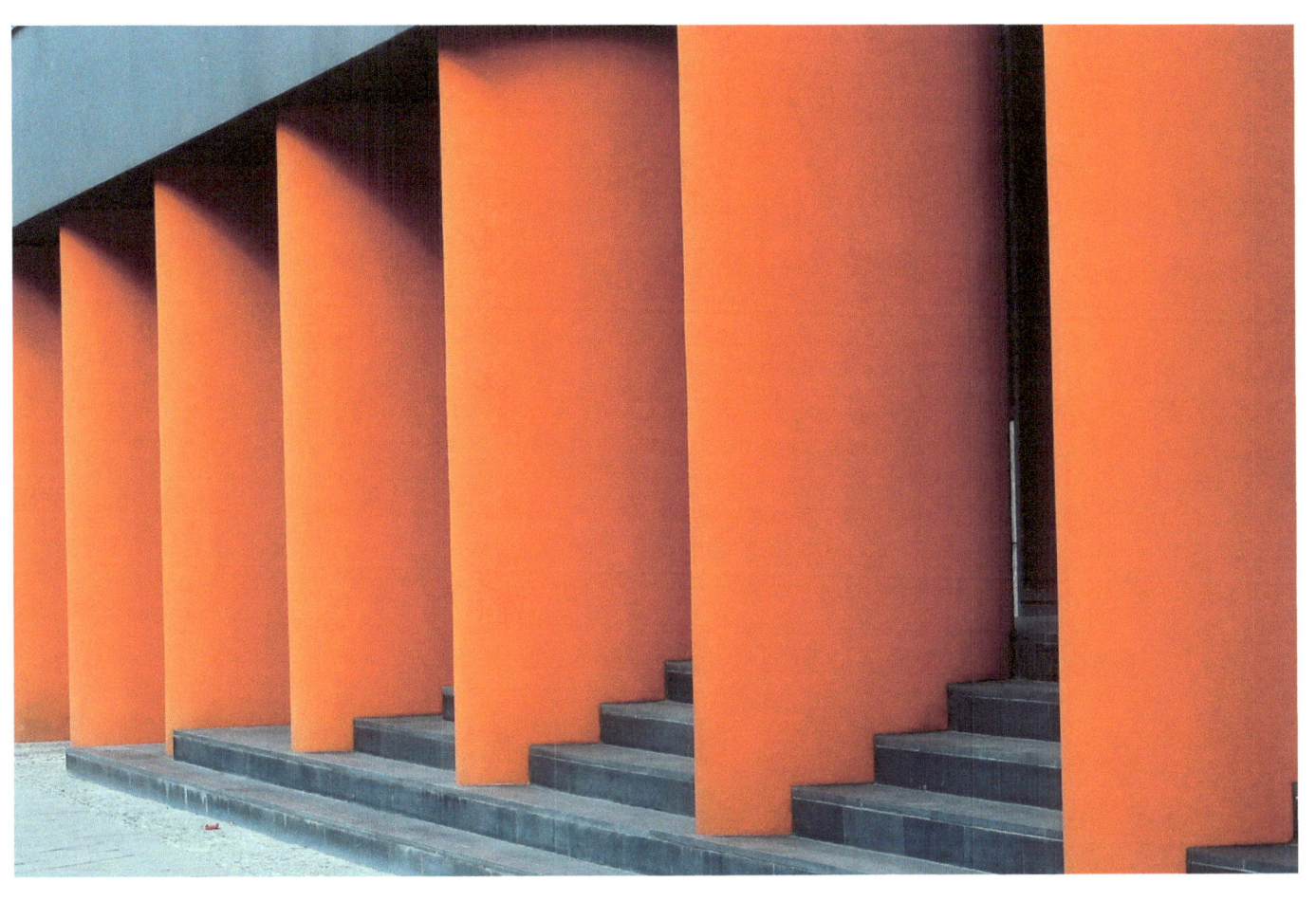

Columns – Berlin

2004, 48" x 72"
C-print on Ultraboard, edition of 5

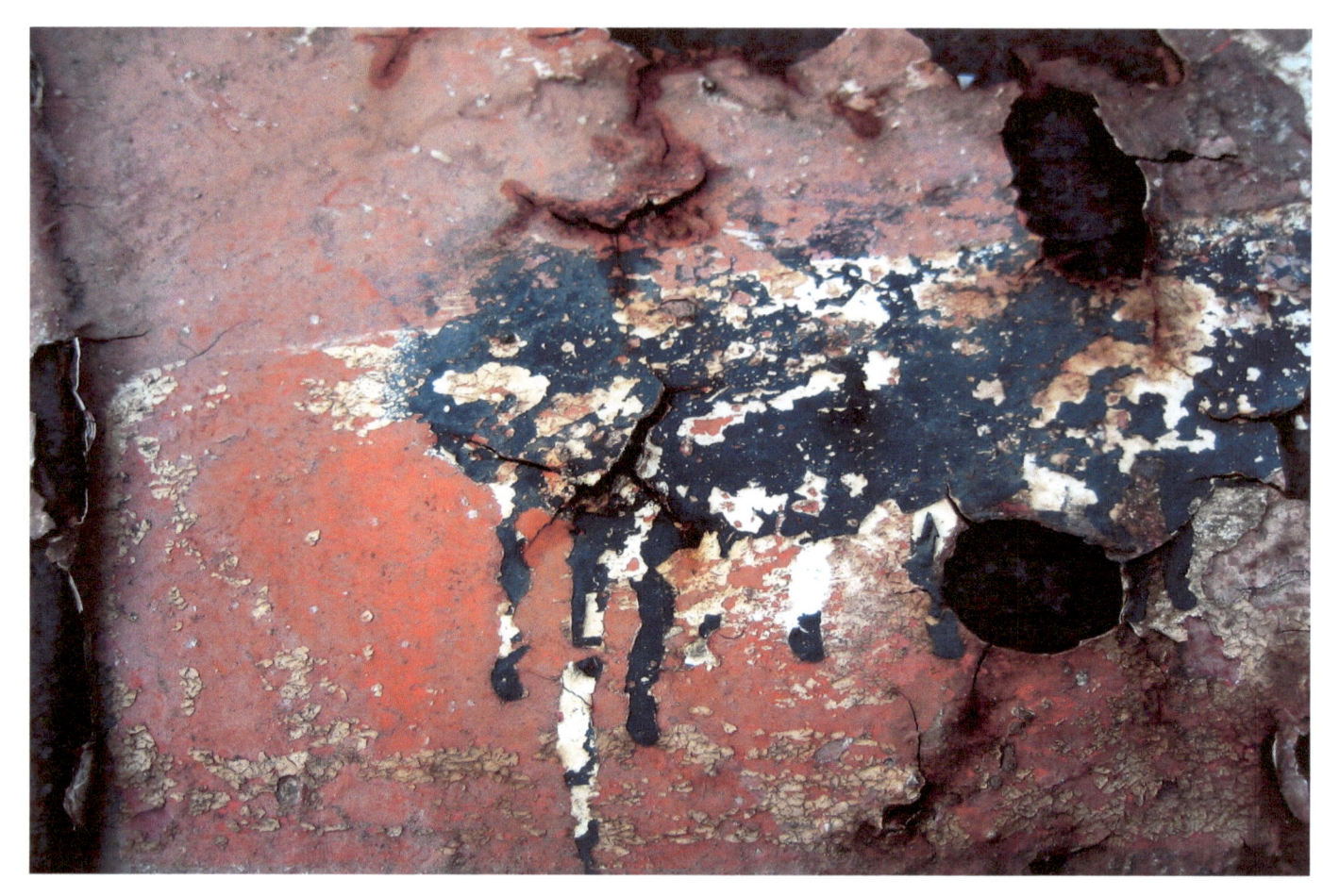

Drip – Los Angeles

2003, 96" x 144". on Four Panels, each 72" x 48",
C-print on Ultraboard, edition of 5

Wally Gilbert's Statement

I began making digital images as art when I discovered that I could make large prints from images taken with a small digital camera and that these prints carried an emotional and asthetic impact. My earliest work was of fragments of the visual world, either portions of natural scenes or of man's architectural or industrial artifacts. My first one-person show included a 48" x 72" image made from a two-megapixel camera.

I was invited to Poland, by Jan Kubasiewicz and Josef Piwkowski, to do an installation at the Norblin Site in Warsaw. These photographs of decaying machinery were installed in Warsaw in the Summer of 2007 as twenty-six 12' x 8' hangings and thirty 36" x 24" prints, face-mounted on plexiglas. This show was exhibited again in Lodz and in Poznan.

After photographing dancers in the ballet, I went on to explore abstractions, first in a "Vanishing" series, that was based on a natural form, the outline of a human head. The many patterns produced in that series all shared some aspect of a biological or natural curve, which still was manifest even in the smallest cropping of those images.

In my later work the basic element was a straight, shaded line, which I used to create geometric patterns. The "Geometric Series" explored patterns in color or black-and-white created from overlapping squares or triangles or just from lines, taken either simply or in intersecting groups.

I make many images by hand on the computer. The computer simply holds the intermediate forms as I superpose the many layers I create to build up the image. The images begin in black and white, and then I color them in the computer. I generate these colors either by accessing the colors available or, in a more complicated fashion, by using the ability to change the global input-output functions for each color and intensity separately. When the layers containing the colored images interact with each other, still more color patterns appear. The computer is a digital workspace, driven by my hand and eye.

My most recent work involves photographs moved to extreme values in color space yielding strange color contrasts further superimposed on each other. These images exemplify my delight in light and form, and my search for a three-dimensional effect on a two-dimensional surface. I search for depth beyond the picture plane and for mystery.

Wally Gilbert's Biography

Wally Gilbert had a long international career as a scientist, working in Molecular Biology on genes and DNA. He was awarded a Nobel Prize in Chemistry, in 1980, for solving the mystery of DNA sequencing. Fred Sanger in England and Gilbert in the United States shared that prize for finding ways to decipher the order of chemical groups along the DNA molecule and hence to make it possible for the first time to read the genes. Those discoveries drove the development of Biology as a gene-based science across the last four decades and led to the working out of the Human Genome program and the current understanding of all organisms.

For the last seventeen years Gilbert has been working in Digital Art. He began by making large images of fragments of the world, focusing on form, texture, and color, using a small digital camera. Very often these pictures were drawn from machines or from architecture. Jan Kubasiewicz, a professor at the Massachusetts College of Art, saw his work and organized his first one-person exhibition in 2004. He was invited to Poland, by Kubasiewicz and Jozef Zuk Piwkowski, to create an installation at the Norblin Site in Warsaw, an old decaying factory. This installation, consisting of twenty-six 12' by 8' hangings and thirty 36" x 24" prints face-mounted on Plexiglas, was installed at Norblin in Warsaw for two months in 2007 and then later that year in Łodz and again in Poznan in 2009. The set of thirty face-mounted prints were also exhibited in New York, Washington D.C., Los Angeles, and San Diego.

Gilbert was invited to participate in creating a book on the Boston Ballet Company. He spent several years photographing ballet dancers in rehearsal. These pictures, which capture the joy and motion of the dancers, appeared in a book on that company "Behind the Scenes at Boston Ballet" by Christine Temin with 68 pictures by Wally Gilbert.

Gilbert then moved to abstractions, first based on silhouettes derived from photographs, then to ever more abstract images based on the human head, at first still interpretable, but later in patterns having only a slight residual aspect of a biological curve. Then he created digital images, made by hand on the computer, based on geometrical forms. This work involved patterns of superimposed shrinking squares and triangles, strongly colored or in black and white, and led finally to images involving single lines. Most recently he has been exploring abstractions created by superimposing several photographic images.

Wally Gilbert

Selected Solo Exhibitions

"Retrospective," LabCentral, Cambridge, MA	2018
"Towers," Viridian Gallery, Chelsea, NYC	2017
"Doors to Nowhere,' Salon R, Cambridge, MA	2017
"Broken City," Khaki Gallery, Boston, MA	2016
"Journeying," Permanent exhibition, AGH University, Krakow, Poland	2016--
"Broken City" Viridian Gallery, Chelsea, NYC	2016
"Patterns & Recognition," Seoul National University Bundang Hospital, curated by Chang and Jae Kim	2015-2016
"Transformations," Viridian Artists, Chelsea, NYC	2014
"Patterns & Recognition," The Howard Hughes Medical Institure, Janelia Farm, VA	2014
"Wally Gilbert," CJ Gallery, Art San Diego 2013, San Diego, CA	2013
"Wally Gilbert: A Room of Light," Milton Art Museum, Canton, MA	2013
"Wally Gilbert: Black & White," Khaki Gallery, Boston, MA	2013
"Digital Constellations," Lindau City Museum, Lindau, Germany	2013
"Wally Gilbert: New Black and White Images," Viridian Artists, Chelsea, NYC	2013
"Wally Gilbert", CJ Gallery, Art San Diego 2012, San Diego, CA	2012
"En-Lighten," Khaki Gallery, Boston, MA	2012
"Journeying," The Artemis Gallery, Krakow, Poland, curated by Wieslawa Piotrowska-Sowadska	2012
"Pattern & Recognition," The Art Gallery, Antelope Valley College, Lancaster, CA	2012
"Squares, Triangles, and Lines," Galerie im Einstein, Berlin	2011
"Projekt Norblin," New Art Wet Music Foundation, Bydgoszcz, Poland	2011
"Squares and Triangles," Viridian Artists, Chelsea, NYC	2011
"Vanishing," CJ Gallery, San Diego, CA	2010
"Vanishing Profiles," Khaki Gallery, Boston, MA	2010
"The Norblin Project and Other Images," CJ Gallery and OCIO DESIGN GROUP, San Diego,CA	2010
"Wally@Wainwright," Wainwright Bank, Cambridge, MA	2010
"Vanishing," BAAK Gallery, Cambridge, MA	2009
Norblin Installation, Poznan, Poland, curated by Jan Kubasiewicz and Zuk Piwkowski	2009
"The Norblin Project and other Images," CJ Art Gallery, San Diego, CA	2009
"IN COLOR & BEYOND," Khaki Gallery, Boston, MA	2009
"Fresh Fruit," Mayyim Hayyim Gallery, Newton, MA	2009
"Stillness and Motion," Viridian Artists, Chelsea, NYC	2008
"LEEKS & CHAINS," Khaki Gallery, Wellesley, MA	2008
"The Norblin Project and other Images," CJ Art Gallery, San Diego, CA	2007
BAAK Gallery, Cambridge, MA	2007
Norblin Installation, Galeria PATIO,Lodz, Poland, curated by Zuk Piwkowski, Jan Kubasiewicz, and Aurelia Mandziuk	2007
Norblin Site Installation, Warsaw, Poland, curated by Jan Kubasiewicz and Zuk Piwkowski	2007
"The Norblin Project: Images of Decay," American Center for Physics, College Park, MD	2007
"IN COLOR," Khaki Gallery, Wellesley, MA	2007
"The Norblin Project: Images of Decay," LACDA, Los Angeles, CA	2006
"The Norblin Project: Images of Decay," Viridian Artists, Chelsea, NYC	2006
Jock Colville Hall, Churchill College, University of Cambridge, Cambridge, UK	2006
Ann Janss Gallery, Los Angeles, CA	2005
Doran Gallery, Massachusetts College of Art, Boston, MA, curated by Jan Kubasiewicz	2004

Wally Gilbert Websites

http://wallygilbert.com
http://wallygilbertscarves.com

www.ingramcontent.com/pod-product-compliance
Lightning Source LLC
Chambersburg PA
CBHW051100180526
45172CB00002B/717